Bits of Fashion
Stories, Interviews, Reviews

Victoria West

Bits of Fashion
Stories, Interviews, Reviews

Victoria West

ISBN: 9781492316343
Photo credit (front cover, back cover): Victoria West
Front cover image: Swarovski jewelry and accessories featured
at Swarovski Fashion Suite for Toronto International Film
Festival at Shangri-La Hotel in Toronto, Canada, September
2012

Official website:
www.FashionStyleBeautyandMore.blogspot.com

To my family, with love

My dear reader,

I hope you'll enjoy reading this book as much as I enjoyed writing it. I started writing about fashion in 2010 when I was on my maternity leave, while taking care of my baby son, and haven't stopped ever since. My first incursion into the Canadian fashion world was through the blog "Fashion, Style, Beauty and More" that I founded in February 2010. But the blog was never my purpose, the blog was merely the means to arrive here – to write the book that you are holding in your hands right now and to share it with you. While my blog was a journey, an exciting one at that, this book was a destination that has always called me, never letting me give up to write.

"Bits of Fashion" is a collection of essays, interviews and reviews that I have written and published on my blog *Fashion, Style, Beauty and More.blogspot.com* since 2010. In this book you will read some of the stories that inspired me; interviews with Canadian designers, professionals from the fashion industry, artists; as well as book reviews.

I love to write, I love fashion, and I love to write about fashion. I live and breathe fashion, and now I am happy to bring it to you in this book. Come with me into an amazing, exciting and fabulous world seen through my eyes and my senses, and let me share with you some fashion insights that are worth knowing. I invite you to be a part of my fashion universe and to witness with me all that this fascinating world of dazzle, glamour and beauty has to offer.

Victoria West,
Toronto

Contents

Part I

FASHION STORIES

Little Black Dress

There are some fashion pièces de resistance which shouldn't be missing from anyone's wardrobe, and the little black dress is one of them.

As everybody knows, the little black dress, or LBD, is usually an elegant black dress of a simple yet chic design, which is an evening or a cocktail dress, a dress appropriate to be worn in many different occasions. Most of the times it's short, knee-long, or under-knee-long. It can be styled up or down, depending on the occasion, and depending if said occasion is during day or evening. For instance, it can be worn with a blazer or a jacket for a day occasion, like work, or a job interview; but it also can be worn with prominent jewelry, pearls or other accessories for an evening occasion like a party, going out to a restaurant, and so on.

Historically, it goes back to Coco Chanel, and has lasted throughout decades ever since. Coco Chanel invented the little black dress as a must have universal garment in any woman's wardrobe. It was designed to be suitable and affordable for any woman, regardless of her social class, educational background or financial means. It was also conceived to be of a simple design, so it can be worn for years instead of one single fashion season. Being part of a specific trend would mean for the little black dress to go out of style as soon as that trend would go away; so instead, it was supposed to be kept as simple as possible, in order for it to be "in" for the next and next fashion seasons to come. And so, the little black dress survived decades and decades after its creator was gone, and today, just like almost one hundred years ago, it is still a must have in any woman's wardrobe.

Nowadays, the little black dress is more than just a piece of garment, it's a concept. Since it was created by Coco Chanel in 1926, it inspired many other fashion designers, beauty creators, artists. The most memorable little black dress in history is the one designed by Hubert de Givenchy and worn by Audrey Hepburn in the film "Breakfast at Tiffany's" (1961). In 2001 the little black dress concept inspired Avon Cosmetics to create a new elegant fragrance called Little Black Dress, a perfume that won the Fragrance Foundation Award in 2002.

The little black dress is not missing from my wardrobe either. I bought it in 2006, I love it and I still can wear it without it getting outdated or me getting bored of it. I wore it to such occasions like weddings, christening parties, Valentine's parties and other glam gatherings, and I am ready to wear it again. Each time when I wear it, I like to accessorize it differently, for a new and fresh look, and it actually saved me many times. I remember a particular instance when I was considering wearing a red dress for a glamorous occasion, but when I tried it on just before the event, I decided I didn't really like how it fit me, so in the last minute I made up my mind for my precious little black dress.

How to Attend a Fashion Week

Attending a Fashion Week is a glamorous experience many fashionistas and fashion consumers are very much looking forward to. I am an avid fashion consumer myself, and I am a frequent guest to Toronto Fashion Week. I attended a fashion show at Toronto Fashion Week for the first time in March 2010 (it was a fall collection showed by the Canadian designer Linda Lundstrom), and since then I went to Toronto Fashion Week every year.

If you are looking to attend the Fashion Week in your city, or a specific Fashion Week from another city, the first thing first to do is to seek out that Fashion Week's official website. The website should contain such basic information related to the preparations for the upcoming Fashion Week like contact information, volunteer information, Fashion Week schedule, list of designers presenting their collections during the Fashion Week, buy ticket information, newsletter. Browse all the pages and categories to familiarize yourself with the website and with the steps of the fashion event to come that you want to attend.

Get yourself on the Fashion Week newsletter and you will receive all the information and notifications about the fashion shows.

You could consider volunteering for the Fashion Week, for a closer exposure to the fashion world, for some fashion networking, and why not, for new friends. The website will announce the areas volunteers are needed for. It could be fashion environment, head office administration, décor, event set-up, distributing marketing materials, greeting guests, registration, and other areas. The website will also announce the days and times volunteers are needed.

Once the names of the designers showing their collections during the Fashion Week, as well as the schedule of the shows and buy ticket information, are available on the website, decide what show(s) you want to attend and buy your ticket(s) well in advance if you want to attend the show of a specific designer (or the shows of several designers). Do not leave buying ticket(s) to your favorite show(s) for the last minute, as you could find them sold out. When I first attended Toronto Fashion Week in March 2010, I wanted to see Canadian designer David Dixon's fashion show; but when I got around to buy a ticket, all of them were sold out, so I had to choose another designer's show, Linda Lundstrom's. Do not let that happen to you, if you are looking forward to seeing your favorite designer's collection, and buy your ticket well in advance.

So, you have decided what show(s) you want to attend, you have already purchased the ticket(s). Next step is going to the Fashion Week itself. How to grab a good seat for the show? Don't forget that a fashion show is not a concert, and the space where it takes place is not a huge one, so the seats are limited. It's just the runway and most of the times 6 rows of seats on one side, and 6 rows of seats on the other side. Your seat is guaranteed of course, since you have bought the ticket for the show; but the problem is where to sit for a good view of the collection(s)? Keep in mind that quite a lot of seats are already reserved in the first rows for VIPs, special guests, media, and the consumers and visitors take their seats in the back rows. Unless the seats are numbered and you have a specific seat for the fashion show, regular visitors take theirs seats as per the availability, once the reserved seats are occupied. In this case, the best seat is in the last row, because you could stand, for a better visibility, to watch the show without bothering anybody in your back. Anyone who sits in the middle rows cannot stand to watch the show, because in this case they would bother other consumers. When I first attended Toronto Fashion Week, I sat in the last row, and I am glad I was inspired to do so, because I could stand for a better visibility without bothering others; but people in front of me sitting in the middle rows could not do so.

How to dress for a fashion show? Stylish, of course. It's a glamorous event, so don't hesitate to dress up. Leave your jeans and T-shirts for some more casual occasions, and choose a dressy outfit. The same stands for the make-up and the hairstyling, they should be stunning. As for the hairstyling, you don't necessarily have to go to see a stylist before the fashion show, just make sure you have a good hair day.

Each Spring We Are in Love with Color

Spring is one of the most exciting times of the year. Besides the actual warm weather that all of us have longed for during the cold winter months, it's the time when we go for shopping again, renewing and reinventing our wardrobes, making plans for new outfits, embracing new trends.

My favorite trend for spring is Color Blocking. I love color, I feel inspired by color, I feel I can stand out of the crowd when I wear color. Ever since Color Blocking made its way from runways to stores and then to our wardrobes one Spring-Summer season (remember the colorful 2011?), I hopelessly fell in love with this trend. And I assure you it's not just a casual "fling", it's love for a lifetime. I still can't forget Gucci's Spring-Summer collection from 2011 with its colorful outfits that brought so much life on the runways. My very favorites have been two of Gucci's outfits from the collection that changed the world of fashion for a long time – one of them was the orange blazer with the purple top and emerald green pants, accessorized with the gold belt (Camilla Belle was one of the celebrities who wore that outfit); and the other one was the butterfly dress with the purple top and orange bottom (an outfit that had been preferred by celebrities like Kim Kardashian and Jennifer Lawrence).

This trend inspired me so much, that it made me re-think my entire wardrobe. Like many other people, I have had my years of black and black only, black from head to toe. But that was a long time ago, during my high-school and university years to be more exact, when black was my second nature. But no more – this time, Color Blocking had become my second nature. So what did I do? I didn't buy the Gucci outfits I felt in love with, but I used them as inspiration for my own wardrobe and my own style. That summer you could see me wearing an orange blazer from H&M and a purple sleeved top from Suzy Shier, or some other times a purple strap top from Zara, with dress pants or a pencil skirt. It may not have been the acclaimed Gucci outfit from the runways of Milan, but it made me feel good about myself for the entire year. Needless to say, my friends appreciated and admired my new colorful style.

So it became official – 2011 marked the beginning of the Color Era. Black was sooo last century! Or, I guess we could also say "Color Blocking is the new Black"!

Then the next Fall-Winter season came along, and Color Blocking was still there. Dozens and dozens of exquisite colorful outfits showed off on the fashion runways across the globe – New York, London, Paris, Milan, Toronto. It was unbelievable. Gucci did it yet again, with irresistible outfits in bright colors, and so did many other European and North American designers. Forget about black for winter, it's color time all year long!

Other spring seasons have come and gone since then, each of them with new trends, but Color Blocking has not gone away like many other trends do once their season is over. It's still here, on runways, in fashion and style magazines, in department stores, in our wardrobes. And I want it to stay and stay, because I truly love it. Color Blocking is here for us to brighten our days, both literally and figuratively. And the good thing about it is that you don't have to splurge on too many new and expensive outfits. The beauty of the color trend is that it's so versatile, that you can adapt it using what you already have in your closet. Surely there are many outfits in different colors in one's wardrobe – wear it and enjoy it baby!

Manolo Blahnik Shoes

What is the most desired name in a woman's shoe closet? Ever since "Sex and the City" the TV show started to air in 1998, women around the world started to think shoes differently. Carrie Bradshaw became a fashion symbol for millions of women not only for her crazy yet stylish outfits, but also for her footwear choices, safe to say the most elegant, attractive and coveted shoes ever. Manolo Blahnik became her favorite shoe designer, as well as the favorite shoe name for millions of women across the globe, regardless of their country, profession or background. Whether they can actually afford these exquisite shoes, or only dream of them, a fact remains a fact – Manolo Blahnik is the first footwear designer on women's mind around the world.

And it's easy to understand. You can't blame a woman for buying or for coveting to buy Manolo Blahnik shoes. He's the king of the shoes, so give Caesar what is Caesar's. Fashionistas across the world still remember the Something Blue Satin Pump shoes by Manolo Blahnik which made sensation in the first "Sex and the City" movie, when Carrie wore them on the day she married Mr. Big. These royal blue shoes were specifically designed for the movie. Even though it's been a few years from the first "Sex and the City" film, and even though there was a sequel to the film ("Sex and the City 2"), these shoes still make sensation in Manolo Blanhik boutiques around the world. And speaking of the sequel, they also make their appearance in the second "Sex and the City" movie – they can be seen in Carrie's closet in the Fifth Avenue apartment where she lives with Big.

The classic collection from Manolo Blahnik features some of the well-known designs, worn by Carrie Bradshaw throughout the "Sex and the City" epopee (the TV show as well as the two movies), and it includes shoes like Something Blue Satin Pump, but also Patent Leather Mary Jane shoes which Carrie wore during Season 4 of the TV series or Jeweled Satin d'Orsay shoes which she wore during Season 6.

Jeans: From Working Pants to High Fashion

Jeans are probably the only garment present in absolutely any wardrobe. Also, it's the only garment which would fit absolutely any person. It became indispensable for anyone in our times. While jeans are a casual garment, it means comfort first of all. People wear jeans while working, shopping, going for a walk with the dog in the park, going to a picnic, going to cinema, going to have a beer with their buddies, traveling, partying, and so on. How could you possibly live without jeans, when it's literally impossible to substitute them with anything else?

Jeans have a long history. Initially, they were designed for work, but as the years and decades passed, their use started to extend. They became a very popular casual wear during the fifties, and have been so ever since. Also, they became one of the milestone fashion symbols of the Western world. Now they come in so many different styles – high-waist cut jeans, low-rise jeans, skinny jeans, straight jeans, loose jeans, Capri jeans, and so many more styles. There is the perfect pair of jeans for everyone out there.

Some of the historic brands for jeans are Levi's, Lee and Wrangler. Nowadays, every conceivable fashion brand in the world features jeans, from the cheapest brand to the most expensive designer – you name it, it's there. There are jeans out there for as little as $10, and there are jeans for thousands of dollars – these are not just working pants anymore, they are haute couture.

Reinvent Your Wardrobe

When I was on my maternity leave I didn't have that much time for shopping, as my baby kept me really busy. I tried to go shopping in the mall with the baby a couple of times, but honestly, it was a fairly more difficult adventure than it used to be before my son's birth, of course.

However, I still would go out on weekends with my husband and son – visiting my friends, going to parties, to picnics, to barbeques, and so on, and we would take our son with us all the time. One of my wardrobe rules is "never ever wear the same shirt in the same place". My friends don't really have the chance to see me wearing the same outfit for the second time. But after the birth of my baby I suddenly realized I could go shopping less frequently than I used to go before, although online shopping became a good alternative for me. And what I also realized is that if I wanted to keep my habit to never ever wear the same shirt in the same place, I needed to prove creativity and to be inventive.

So, I had a closer look at my wardrobe. I started thinking that it was a good idea to reinvent my wardrobe – to wear and accessorize clothes and outfits I didn't have the opportunity to wear in a long time. So I started digging, and I discovered that I had quite a few outfits which I hadn't worn for years, and now it was a good time to wear them again. Two big advantages were on my side. First of all, when I buy a new outfit, I choose a garment which is not a part of a very prominent trend. I make my outfit choices following some more classical lines, and this way I can wear those clothes years long. I avoid buying clothes from very specific trends which would go out of style the next fashion season. Instead, all my clothes are wearable for a long time, which saves me money, time and imagination efforts, when it comes to what I should wear tonight. The other advantage was the very fact that I didn't show off these older outfits of mine for a long time, so I could wear them with no worries again. Sometimes new fashion is actually newly discovered old fashion, and an old dress can be just as good as a new one.

I remember a birthday party I attended the summer after my baby was born. That night I decided to wear a Suzy Shier summer floral dress which I bought 3 years earlier. I only wore it two times for other previous occasions, both times during the year when I actually bought it. Since then, it just hung in my walking closed, as I had completely forgotten about it. So when I was getting ready for that party, I decided it was time to wear it again. I was complimented for it, and nobody even realized it was not a new dress.

Another similar experience during my maternity year was with another dress of mine, which was much older. I bought it when I was still a university student, but its classical and simple style resisted throughout the years. For me, it's a vintage dress (even though it's not technically vintage), and I still enjoy wearing it. But there were also times when I literally dumped it in my closed, until the day I decided I should wear it again. So one night I took it out visiting some friends, and one of my friends, who knew me for many years, told me that he remembered this dress. The story of this dress is a bit more special, as it has a sentimental value for me – I was wearing it on the night when I first met my husband (and some of his friends), and he found me very attractive in that dress. Shortly after that we started dating, then the dating turned into a relationship, and now we are married and have a son. That's why I kept the dress for so many years, while I didn't keep other outfits and garments as old as this one. So it didn't surprise me when my friend recognized my dress which I also wore more than 10 years earlier.

Another old outfit in my wardrobe which I thought was worth to be reinvented was a dark blue little suit from Le Chateau. When I first bought it, I wore it about three times during the first few months, but after that, again, I somehow forgot about it and neglected to wear it for a while. I rediscovered it in my wardrobe when I was a stay at home mom and figured I should wear it again, which I most certainly did, to a birthday party, and then to a Christmas party.

I also love to accessorize my old and new outfits alike. Sometimes a piece of jewelry, or a scarf, or another accessory will completely change an outfit, making it look different, or even new.

White for Summer

I love white for summer. It's not only a comfortable color to wear during the hot season, but it's also stylish, fashionable and never out of trends. White is a part of classic, and one will always be able to wear white for summer, no matter what the current trends are.

This being said, it happens that my wardrobe doesn't lack white at all. I fell in love with white one beautiful and hot summer a few years ago, when I decided I should complete my wardrobe with white outfits. I went shopping, and I ended up buying quite a few white garments – a short-sleeved blazer, a top, a shirt, and a handbag (I already had a white clutch in my closet). Then I went on with my white shopping and I bought white dress pants, a pair of pumps, shorts, a skirt, a bolero and a blouse. Finally, I purchased a pair of white stiletto sandals, and voila – my white wardrobe got completed. I was able to wear my white outfits at work, at parties, going shopping, visiting friends, and I still do, considering that a classical fashion garment like a white outfit is wearable for so many occasions.

I like to refresh my white outfits by styling them up with different accessories and jewelry pieces each time, so they won't look the same. Another way I like to accessorize my white clothes is by combining them with pieces in certain hot and attractive colors, like turquoise, purple, mauve, pink.

How I Got My Fashion Inspiration from the Film "The Devil Wears Prada"

When it comes to chick flick movies, besides the fun you have with your girlfriends watching them, I realize they actually are good at something – they can serve as fashion inspiration. I definitely get my inspiration in terms of looks and outfits from chick flick films, and one of my favorites is "The Devil Wears Prada". After I saw this movie for the first time, I started to see fashion differently, and it made me think that I should try a different dress code than I used to do before. It made be want to be more daring in dressing up, to be a bit more extravagant, more elegant than casual. Why not, I was thinking. What's wrong with wearing designer outfits on a daily basis, which would make me stand out of the crowd? Or, not necessarily designer outfits, but some outfits which would make me look different, which would make people notice me?

I know this film was perceived as a controversial one up to some point, due to the high (lack of) morals in the fashion industry it reveals, a.k.a. a million girls who would kill for a crazy and impossibly to accomplish job for the fashion's sake, or first assistants starving themselves to anorexia for a chance to go to Paris Fashion Week. But despite that, I really enjoyed the fashions in this film. I enjoyed watching Andrea Sachs' fashion evolution from the ugly duckling to the beautiful swan. I enjoyed watching her gorgeous outfits throughout the entire movie. My favorite outfit worn by Andrea in "The Devil Wears Prada" is the white Chanel coat that she is depicted wearing on Manhattan streets, on a usual business day. The reason I loved this coat is that I have a similar one, created by British designer

Jane Norman, which I bought in 2005 and which I absolutely adore. It's one of my pièces de resistance and it's a true example of "smart shopping", a piece that holds on for years and years. Despite the fact that I have already worn it for such a long time, it's still in good shape and I am really fond of it. It has a similar style and cut like the Chanel coat from the movie, and although it's not a Chanel, it's not less special to me. I still enjoy wearing it, even though I have had it for all these years.

Shortly after I saw the film "The Devil Wears Prada", I decided I was ready to change my style. I went shopping, and I bought a few outfits which were a bit more extravagant and attention catching than whatever I used to wear before. Sure enough, I started wearing my new outfits to work the following day. My husband noticed the change in my style immediately and said I looked good. A few days later, he noticed that my change in style had become something constant rather than occasional and asked me: "Did you dress like this before, or you actually changed your style after you saw that movie "The Devil Wears Prada"?" And not only did my husband notice my new "up-graded" style, but also so did my co-workers and my friends, which made me feel really special.

Indeed, the film inspired me in terms of courage and daring to look different. I made my decision – no more plain-Jane outfits in my wardrobe. Beauty is not something to be ashamed of, and it shouldn't be considered as such.

Part II

INTERVIEWS

An Interview with Canadian Dancer and Choreographer Tré Armstrong

Tré (Tracy) Armstrong is a well-known TV personality from Toronto, as well as a dancer, choreographer, actress, and judge for the Canadian dancing show "So You Think You Can Dance". Besides her work in front of the TV cameras, she also involves in a number of charitable actions and gives back to the community through dance and performing arts. I met Tré Armstrong for the first time in May 2011, when I attended a charitable fashion show held by Children's Aid Foundation from Toronto. At that time, Children's Aid Foundation launched a new charitable fund named "Ignite the Spark", a fund that honored six Canadian celebrities as "Sparks" – inspirational Canadians who give back. The six celebrities honored by this fund launched by Children's Aid Foundation were Tré Armstrong, Debra McGrath (actress), Colin Mochrie (actor), Andrea Martin (actress), Nick Ugoalah (sportsman) and Arlene Dickinson (marketing professional).

I had the great pleasure of interviewing Tré Armstrong at this exceptional event, when she talked to me about her inspirational work and the charitable projects she got involved in.

***

Victoria West: Tell us more about your involvement in Children's Aid Foundation projects.

Tré Armstrong: In 2010 I was asked by the event producer and the foundation to join their gala team as Creative Director and Choreographer. It was a blast and we were nominated for a few awards too, a great bonus. I think somewhere in between my name was pulled up for consideration for an honoree award as a luminary in entertainment. This was for the Children's Aid Foundation's newest fund, the "Ignite the Spark" Fund, created by Andrea Weissman-Daniels and Mark Daniels. I was more than thrilled to say the least.

Victoria West: What does the Spark honor from Children's Aid Foundation mean to you?

Tré Armstrong: It represents the notion that the path I am on is a positive one, a journey that includes giving back to the community through dance and performing arts. It makes me happy to know people are listening and watching as free dance programs are made available to youth in the community.

Victoria West: You are known as a celebrity giving back to the community. What other similar projects have you been involved in?

Tré Armstrong: Currently, I host a free day of dance called the Give Back. It's back on this summer at the National Ballet

School with over 20 classes to choose from. I also host a free dance program called D-Tour. This is a unique urban dance program for either all-girls or all-boys aged 14-19. Participants get to create their own dance moves while learning from professionals in the dance and entertainment industry, plus their dance is a showcase at the end of the program for close family and friends. This has all led up to the creation of my new not-for-profit foundation called the "Tré Armstrong Give Back" Foundation.

Victoria West: Why do celebrities choose to involve in Children's Aid Foundation projects, as well as other projects alike?

Tré Armstrong: We understand that we are human, just like everyone else, and like other people we too have a past. Our past, at times, pushes us to reach out to family, friends and public organizations for help. Since we have a voice and a platform that others are willing to listen to, we have a duty at times to support foundations that provided help for people in many forms of need. Some of those people may have been us.

Victoria West: You are a judge for "So You Think You Can Dance" show – do you consider it to be a milestone in your dancing career? Has it impacted your career as a professional dancer in any way?

Tré Armstrong: Of course becoming a choreographer and judge on "So You Think You Can Dance" Canada was a milestone, a huge one at that! Coupled with my past work I now have a larger voice that more people listen to and I am thankful to be able to have opened up my not-for-profit foundation and pursue opening up a dance studio/community hub for youth in Brampton, Ontario.

Victoria West: You are also known as being passionate about helping youth to get active. How do you think you impact the lives of the young talented who come to compete at "So You Think You Can Dance" show?

Tré Armstrong: All I know is how to be me: empathetic yet stern. I will always treat others with respect and only ask that others do the same in return by taking in how and what I say/do. I love to develop our future dance monsters. It's a pleasure to watch them grow and it's an honor to be a part of the process. *How* I impact their lives, is out of my hands.

Another Interview with Canadian Dancer and Choreographer Tré Armstrong

My second interview with Canadian TV celebrity Tré Armstrong took place in August 2011 when she launched her new not-for-profit foundation "Tré Armstrong Give Back". The launch event was marked by a fabulous party held at The Spoke Club in Toronto. The mission of the new foundation was clear, to make dance and creative artistic expression accessible to the youth across Canada, that may otherwise not have the opportunity, and to inspire their artistic hopes, dreams and passions. Dance empowers people and Tré Armstrong wanted to give that empowerment to all youth, regardless of their circumstances and in some cases, because of just who they are! The "Tré Armstrong Give Back" Foundation focuses on developing life skills through enjoyable youth programming and performing arts at the community level alongside educational classes and seminars, promoting continued learning along with the development of key life and social skills. The "Tré Armstrong Give Back" Foundation believes every child should be allowed to explore their inner "spirit of dance".

***

Victoria West: How did the idea of the "Tré Armstrong Give Back" Foundation appear?

Tré Armstrong: In 2007 I rented a dance studio for 3 hours, held three classes and had 30 participants. And it was all for free! I figured there was something to this, and at Christmas in

2009 I held another event called "Give Back", giving a full day of free dance classes while raising money and food for charity. Now, in 2011, we just finished our fourth "Give Back" event, with over 400 kids, 25 dance and movement classes and so much more!

Victoria West: What were the steps you had to take to start and launch the foundation?

Tré Armstrong: Talk to a lot of people who have opened up a foundation in the past that are still successful, as well as speak to those already in the not-for-profit sector to find out the DOs and DON'Ts. Then, assembling my Board of Directors, Executive Director and pillars of the foundation came next. After that, legalizing was the final first step, of many more to come I assume (laughs).

Victoria West: Who helped you along the process?

Tré Armstrong: All my Board of Directors, Executive Director, current youth dance program participants, my mother, brothers and family, close friends, many volunteers and of course God.

Victoria West: You dedicate your work to children and youth. How will they benefit from the "Tré Armstrong Give Back" Foundation?

Tré Armstrong: We will have free dance programming across Canada for youth ages 7+. Our foundation's mission is to make performing arts more accessible to our nation's future leaders. Our aim is to make available scholarships and awards for various areas of dance and their performance artists and artistic institutions.

Victoria West: Are there any criteria by which children and youth to benefit from the "Tré Armstrong Give Back" Foundation will be selected?

Tré Armstrong: A non-biased selection format will be used at all times.

Victoria West: What are the objectives of the "Tré Armstrong Give Back" Foundation in the near future?

Tré Armstrong: To continue the "Give Back" event at Canada's National Ballet School in Toronto and expand it across Canada, host a national youth dance event to increase awareness to the fact that dance saves lives and raise money to continue youth initiatives such as D-Tour, an urban dance program run in underserved communities.

Victoria West: In the long run, what are your expectations and what do you hope to accomplish with the "Tré Armstrong Give Back" Foundation?

Tré Armstrong: Continued financial support is what is needed at this point in order to bring dance and performing arts programming to places like Winnipeg, Halifax, Brampton and Calgary. We really want this foundation to solidify its synergetic work with various partners in the community at large so that we can continue to bring more free youth programming to areas across Canada that truly need and deserve the engagement. Dance saves lives, literally, and I am living proof.

An Interview with Debbie Wright, Style Expert at Value Village

Many people find themselves reluctant faced with the idea of thrift shopping, but this fashion segment can be very rewarding. Thrift shopping is not only about merchandise at low prices, but it's also about a great and unique style, a style that can make you stand out of the crowd, a style that won't be copied by anyone else.

When we say thrift shopping in North America, the first place that comes to our mind is Value Village. Debbie Wright is a style expert at Value Village, as well a fashion stylist and confidence builder at Project Closet, a fashion consultancy company. I had the opportunity of interview Debbie in April 2011, when she shared tips and ideas on great thrift shopping.

***

Victoria West: How long have you been in this business?

Debbie Wright: I have been in the fashion/wardrobe business for over 25 years; I established my fashion consulting business, Project Closet, in 1997.

Victoria West: How do you acquire and select the merchandise for the store? Do you follow a specific guidance when selecting the merchandise?

Debbie Wright: Every Value Village store has a nonprofit partner, and those partners ask people in the community to donate gently used items. Value Village pays the nonprofit partners for everything donated to the store. Then, Value Village team members sort through every item and only the highest quality reusable items make it to the floor. Each Value Village has over 100,000 items on the floor at any given time, and they go through roughly 5,000 items every day.

Victoria West: Do people find shopping in a thrift store overwhelming? If yes, what makes them reluctant in becoming Value Village customers?

Debbie Wright: I do hear from time to time that many people find thrift shopping overwhelming due to the large amount of inventory and selection. Value Village merchandises their inventory by category i.e. jackets, then by size. Merchandising this way makes it easier for the shopper to find great fashion pieces.

I also recommend my THRIFT SHOPPING 101 strategy:

First, shop by choosing a category. For example, jackets. Once in jackets, comb through the different types. Think about what you need a jacket for; meaning do you need a nice blazer for work, a denim jacket to go with a cute dress you just got, or a warm outdoor jacket.

Second, remember that vintage sizes are different. When you are thrift shopping make sure to look at sizes above and below what you normally wear. You might just find a great vintage Chanel piece that is labeled as two sizes too big, but that fits you because of the vintage sizing.

Third, try not to get overwhelmed. Thrift stores, especially Value Village stores, have a lot of merchandise to look through. Make sure you wear comfortable shoes and clothes you can easily change out of.

Finally, keep your eyes open and try on everything. Thrift stores are a creative person's dream. You have to be willing to try on anything and everything that looks semi-interesting. Let's say you find a great purple shirt, but it's a purple you normally wouldn't wear. You're reluctant to even try it on, but then you do and you can't imagine your life without it.

Victoria West: Once they had their first shopping experience at Value Village, do customers tend to come back?

Debbie Wright: Absolutely, shoppers become addicted to the "hunt". Thrift shopping is one of the most EXCITING ways to shop. You never know what treasure awaits you at any of the Value Village stores. They add tons of new merchandise to the floor daily. Most customers can't drive by a store without stopping in to take a quick peak and they LOVE to talk about their finds.

Victoria West: What are the greatest advantages of thrift shopping, aside from the low cost of the merchandise? Why would a fashion consumer become a constant Value Village customer?

Debbie Wright: There are many advantages of thrift shopping. Having great style does NOT have to cost a lot of money. When you thrift shop, you have an opportunity to shop for high quality classic items like trench coats, black skirts, white blouses and wrap dresses as well as many unique pieces from vintage jewelry to designer shoes. Your style should express your personality and thrift store shopping finds are endless. The styles found often at the malls are all the same. Thrift opens up an avenue of flair and creativity.

Victoria West: Do you shop at Value Village? If yes, can you give us a few examples of some of your greatest finds?

Debbie Wright: I shop weekly at many of my local Savers stores. Value Village is owned by Savers, Inc. and the stores in most of the US are called Savers. I have found Marc Jacobs classic pumps that were under $30, Diane Von Furstenberg wrap dresses, and vintage Chanel handbags. Most recently, I found a David Meister dress and it's perfect for a Kentucky Derby Show I have – it was only $12.99. I have also found many pairs of designer brand jeans like Citizens of Humanity and Seven for All Mankind for $39.99.

Victoria West: Can you share tips on how to build a great style with what Value Village has to offer?

Debbie Wright: You can stay on trend shopping thrift and I recommend "Making Your Own Mannequin". When you shop, bring pictures of outfits and looks from your favorite, current fashion magazines. They can often be duplicated shopping thrift for much less money.

We also recommend shopping with specific items in mind, for example two new pairs of updated jeans for your wardrobe. Find a pair that fits and flatters your shape today. Choose one darker wash denim that can be dressed up or down and it should be a little longer to accommodate a heel. The other pair should be lighter and long enough to wear with flats. Value Village offers a wonderful versatility in your closet.

An Interview with Dale Debusschere, Manager of Value Village Store in Mississauga, Ontario

My second interview with a Value Village representative took place in October 2011. This time, I talked to Dale Debusschere, manager of a new Value Village store that opened its doors in Mississauga, Ontario, during that very month.

***

Victoria West: How and when did you get involved in the Value Village business?

Dale Debusschere: In late 1993, early 1994, while working as a factory rep for an automotive supply company in Calgary, I met the store manager and district manager at a Value Village store near my company's warehouse. Over the next few months I became convinced that Value Village was the type of company I'd like to join and have been with Value Village since March, 1994.

Victoria West: Why did you choose Mississauga for a new Value Village location in Greater Toronto Area?

Dale Debusschere: Toronto overall is a really important market for Value Village. We have fantastic nonprofit partners, and we have tremendously supportive shoppers. In general, though, when looking at new markets, we typically look at certain geographical areas where both Value Village and our nonprofit partners can be successful in serving local communities. Our other Mississauga store is doing very well, and we feel that the community can support and will love having a second store in the area.

Victoria West: Did the sales go as you expected on these first days since you opened the new store to the public? Or was it lower or higher than your expectations?

Dale Debusschere: We were really proud of our opening weekend, and the response from local shoppers exceeded our expectations. There was definitely excitement in the community leading into our grand opening weekend!

Victoria West: The new fall-winter fashion season has just begun and everybody is shopping for a new fall wardrobe. How does Value Village stand out among traditional retailers (i.e. malls, outlets) to attract customers and keep them, aside from the low prices?

Dale Debusschere: Some of the latest fall-winter trends for 2011 are perfect for thrift shopping, and we love to help our shoppers take the in-season looks and make them their own – for a fraction of the cost to buy new. We even post a guide to seasonal trends on our website. Some of the ones we've observed right now are animal print, faux fur, timeless plaid, and deep jewel tones.

Victoria West: For some of the fashion consumers the label name is also important. What does Value Village have to offer in terms of designer merchandise?

Dale Debusschere: One of the best parts about shopping at Value Village is the thrill of the hunt. Whenever someone shops at our store, they can count on finding a hidden gem, whether it's a designer vintage coat or a designer blouse with the price tag still attached. We have more than 100,000 items on our sales floor, with 5,000 new pieces added daily – so every time you visit you will find something new and unique!

Victoria West: Do you shop at Value Village? If yes, can you give us a few examples of some of your favorite finds?

Dale Debusschere: Yes, I love shopping at Value Village! Being size XLT, I rarely find my "style" of clothing in a traditional retail store because my size selection is quite limited. Big and tall stores typically have a great selection of professional clothing, but the casual styles rarely appeal to me. With Value Village's wide selection of styles, I know it's just a matter of time before I'll find the perfect item. I do have to admit that after nearly 18 years, closet space has become an issue for me. I don't seem to be able to part with (or donate) my finds as quickly as I buy.

Victoria West: Do you encourage your friends and family to thrift shop at Value Village? If yes, are they willing to, or have they already become Value Village customers?

Dale Debusschere: Yes, my family and friends shop at Value Village. I talk about all of the interesting things I find at work so much that it's inspired them to shop at Value Village even more! My friends are especially shopping at Value Village now because of Halloween right around the corner. One of my friends is going to be a zombie and he found everything he needed for his costume at Value Village for under $15! Another of my friends is planning to be Black Swan for Halloween. She found a corset, a tutu, ballet slippers, and gloves for less than $20 – she mixed new accessories and gently used items for this great costume.

Victoria West: Are there any plans for Value Village to open new stores in other GTA locations in the future? And in Canada?

Dale Debusschere: We have a few more stores opening in Canada this year with one in Orillia, Ontario, and another in Yorkton, Saskatchewan, next month. But next year is also going to be a busy year with quite a few new stores opening in the U.S. and Canada, so stay tuned!

An Interview with Singer and Songwriter Jewell

I never met R&B singer and songwriter Jewell, but I had the opportunity to speak with her over the phone in October 2011 (while I was in Toronto and she was in US), when her Public Relations representative from Toronto facilitated a phone interview with the artist for me. At that time Jewell was preparing for two new projects to launch that same fall – the release of her autobiographical book "My Blood, My Sweat, My Tears", as well as the soundtrack with the same name; but also her album "Jewell" produced by the recording company WIDE Awake.

***

Victoria West: When did you know that you wanted to sing?

Jewell: I would say it was in the church. I started singing in the church when I was a little girl, and my mom always said that I was a very eccentric little girl, 'cause all I did was sing, and sing, and sing, and sing; and anybody who knew me and met me would say the same, whether it was at the grocery store, or in the supermarket, or in the church. I've always had the desire and the passion to sing. When I was 3 years old, I did my first solo, and it kind of took off from there, and then I got involved in a couple of musical projects.

We moved from Chicago to Los Angeles in 1979, and I joined there a performing art troupe, where I got a chance to perform. So it's always been a passion that I had, and it started in the church.

Victoria West: When did your career as a professional singer and songwriter begin?

Jewell: My first professional recording was when I recorded a song with Bobby Jimmy and the Critters, it was called "Plastic Women – Plastic Man", and it was my first introduction into the studio; that was one of the first studio sessions I had. Then I recorded a song with L.A. Drinking, and then it went on and on. When I was in my last year in high school, there was a place in L.A. called Modern Memory Lane, where you would go and perform and showcase your talent. Dr. Dré was there one night, and one of my closest friends Michelle, whom I used to call my cousin, knew him from a club called Ease after Dark. She told him that I sang, and he said: "Oh yeah? Let me hear you!" He chose me at the time to work with him. We went down to the studio and we recorded a song, which actually was my first hit. It was a really big underground hit; it couldn't be played on the radio because of the lyrical content, but that was my first major hit and it kicked off my career as a singer and songwriter.

Victoria West: What inspires you as an artist?

Jewell: Good music inspires me. People used to think that I was crazy because I can hear a track, and then within 15 minutes I can write a complete song, with verses. I used to tell people that the music talks to me (laughs), and they thought I was crazy. But I have a big connection with music, and the melody. I started writing poetry when I was probably about 10 or 11 years old, so I would take some of those old poems and pull the best from them and turn this old poetry into new songs.

Victoria West: Among your songs or albums, do you have a favorite one, and if yes, what makes it your favorite?

Jewell (laughs): As far as the songs that have been released to the public, I would have to say my favorite song would probably be the song with me and Aaron Hall "Gonna Give It to Ya", and I had a crazy experience recording that song... I would sing it over and over and over again, and it never gets old. As far as the unreleased material, the WIDE Awake album that is about to be released in November (a solo album of all Jewell songs), there is a song called "Recognize". When I first met the producer, and I first listened to the soundtrack, it was the best music I have ever heard in a long, long time. And he and I, we sort of clicked, we had a "chemistry", so we did an album of 16 songs within a two-week time. This song, "Recognize", it's going to be released on the album that WIDE Awake is going to drop, so people will get the chance to hear it. It's a really beautiful song, and it talks about a famous girl that meets a guy and he is looking at her, and he is afraid to get involved in a relationship with her because he is scared of the Hollywood life. It's an interesting story, and I think that every song tells a story. It's not just a song, it's a story.

Victoria West: Can you tell us more about your album and book "My Blood, My Sweat, My Tears"?

Jewell: "My Blood, My Sweat, My Tears" is an autobiographical book. I also did a soundtrack for the book, "My Blood, My Sweat, My Tears" as well. There are 6 solo songs of myself in this soundtrack, and the songs for the soundtrack reflect the pain that's in the book. It is about my life – I had problems with abuse, I wasn't able to sing, I went to jail, and Death Row Records was a major change in my life.

An Interview with Canadian Singer and Songwriter Anastasia A

I met Canadian singer and songwriter Anastasia A during an audition event that she held at Rehearsal Factory in Toronto in February 2012. Guitarists, drummers, bassists and other musicians came to Rehearsal Factory on that day to compete for an opportunity to join Anastasia and her band and to expand their musical career. Also, the artist was about to release her new single "Kiss and Tell" in just a few days. While interviewing Anastasia, she told me about her plans, her next career moves, and of course about her new song "Kiss and Tell".

***

Victoria West: Can you please tell me about today's event and what are you doing here, what do you want to do after today's auditions?

Anastasia A: Today we are doing our official auditions, so we are auditioning band members for my tour or for my shows. I'm hoping to leave here with some amazing band members, that I'll be taking on tour with me, and we're just looking for a lot of different people and releasing my new single "Kiss and Tell" on Tuesday [February 14th, 2012].

Victoria West: How many new members are you looking for?

Anastasia A: We're looking for a drummer, a bassist, a guitarist, a keyboard man, and one acoustic guitarist for some lighter shows – five people.

Victoria West: When are you going to decide upon the winners?

Anastasia A: It's going to be so hard to pick, but it should take me maybe a week or two. We can't take too long because we have to start prepping for the Canadian Music Week, and they do have to learn 5 to 6 new songs of mine; so we are definitely going to pick them within a week.

Victoria West: How about your new single "Kiss and Tell"?

Anastasia A: I'm so excited about it. It's out on Tuesday February 14th, and it's such a great song, it's so upbeat and fun and I can't wait for everyone to have access to it, because I've been talking about it for so long and no one was able to find it anywhere, so it finally will be available on Tuesday.

Victoria West: Where can your fans buy it or listen to it?

Anastasia A: They can find it on iTunes. Also, we're doing an official remix for a radio edit, so I'm working with MC Flipside from PBR Recordings. He's such a great DJ and house music producer, and he's going to do a very-very nice radio edit. So, we're getting the song on iTunes, then radio edit, and then hopefully on Much Music.

Victoria West: What is the message you send out with this single?

Anastasia A: This single is about relationships. When you meet someone new and you really like them, it would be nice not to go and tell around to everyone about it, but just enjoy the relationship and be a strong person about it. I'm saying that because I know a lot of instances when you meet a new guy, let's say in school or out there – you meet him and you really like him, but then he goes around and tells everyone!

Victoria West: That's not nice!

Anastasia A: No, that's not nice, not classy at all, right? So that's my message – to not kiss and tell, and just be a good person and be confident in your relationships.

Victoria West: Where did the inspiration for this single come from?

Anastasia A: It came from my previous break-up. I had a very serious relationship go downhill a long time ago... well, last summer (giggles), and it comes from my previous relationship experience. So I want to share it with other females – you have to be strong, you have to tough it out.

Victoria West: When did you know for the first time that you wanted to become a singer?

Anastasia A: When I was born (laughs). Except I didn't think I could do it for a while. I took school very seriously, and post-secondary education was very important in my life. When I finished that, I decided to just go forward with my music career. Now I'm just going all the way and I'm actually able to live the dream. It was hard. I would spend 8 hours a day on Internet, Facebook, MySpace and all those different social and media networks. There is lots of going on out there, I had to go out there to some scary people who were on the top and say: "Hey, I'm Anastasia, how do I get into the circle of people who've made it, I want to make it, let's do it". So it was a lot of hassle, a lot of work, a lot of interacting, but finally I'm here, and I'm really excited.

An Interview with Australian Music Band "A Broken Silence"

Australian hip-hop and rock band "A Broken Silence" ("Torcha" John Chmielewski, "B-Don" Brendon Costello, "Cactus" Daniel Bartulovich, "Boots" Simon Lennon and Nathan Tuffin) launched their self-titled album "A Broken Silence" with 13 never heard before songs on March 13th 2012. I interviewed the band in May 2012 and had them share about their newly released album.

***

Victoria West: Please tell us a bit about the band, how it was created and what is your mission?

A Broken Silence: The band started in 2006, just 5 friends making music. We were all from different backgrounds of music that all seemed to gel really well so we started putting together a few experimental rock/hip hop tracks and the band grew from there.

Victoria West: What is the story behind your new album "A Broken Silence"?

A Broken Silence: The new album changed direction a little bit lyrically as we started to write more about our own lives and everyday situations. This album is a little more rock too – raw production and melodic hooks, etc. Our guitarist Cactus (Daniel Bartulovich) now sings on the second LP.

Victoria West: What are your expectations once this album is out there?

A Broken Silence: We would love to do a world tour and are hoping the album gets a good enough response to justify it within the next 12 months.

Victoria West: How do your fans react to your music and what do you think your music means to them?

A Broken Silence: We really hope that they like it.

Victoria West: Do you plan to give concerts or involve in music events in Toronto in the near future?

A Broken Silence: We would love to play shows in Toronto! We hope our music will take us there.

Victoria West: What is your next big project?

A Broken Silence: A new album is in the works. We are always writing and have plenty in the bag, the focus at the moment though is the current release and that it goes well enough for support with a follow up album. We would love to record a new album in Toronto, maybe kill two birds with one stone and play a few shows while we are there.

An Interview with Canadian Designer
Christopher Bates

I saw Canadian fashion designer Christopher Bates for the first time at World MasterCard Toronto Fashion Week in October 2012. He was sitting across of me, with a friend, at a fashion show we both attended. This is when I found out that he was one of the designers showing his new collection at Toronto Fashion Week. A few days later, once the Fashion Week was over, I contacted him and requested an interview, to which he kindly agreed, and we met for our interview during the following week. We talked about his brand, about his newly showed collection, as well as about his plans for the future.

Christopher Bates is one of the leading menswear designers in Canada. Born and raised in Vancouver, he studied fashion design in Milan. Currently, his fashion brand is established in Toronto, retailing at Gotstyle menswear store, among other fine clothing stores.

One of the highlights of his fashion career up until 2012, when this interview was recorded, was his being among the 8 finalists at Mercedes Benz Start Up Program, a prestigious fashion competition for emerging designers, founded in Canada in 2011. The program is sponsored by Mercedes Benz Canada Inc. and is produced in association with Fashion Design Council of Canada (FDCC). The 2012 Semifinal of Mercedes Benz Start Up Program took place in Ottawa, in August 2012, and the Final of this competition took place in Toronto, during Word MasterCard Toronto Fashion Week of October 2012.

***

Victoria West: Please tell us a bit about your brand and its history.

Christopher Bates: I'll start at the beginning – I studied fashion design in Milan, at Istituto Marangoni, in 2006-2007. Then I moved back to Vancouver to start my line, in 2008. I moved to Toronto in 2010 to grow the business, I've been here just over 2 years now, and it's really starting to catch on.

Victoria West: How would you describe the man who wears Christopher Bates designs?

Christopher Bates: It's interesting – when I launched, I was after the 25 to 35-year old crowd; but I've actually found the guys who were 35 to 55 range. So it's the middle age, career oriented guys who appreciate designer fashion.

Victoria West: You were one of the finalists of Mercedes Benz Start Up fashion competition, what do you think being a part of this contest will bring to your fashion career?

Christopher Bates: Mercedes Benz Start Up has been great. We had a chance to meet with a lot of really great industry professionals. They have been mentoring me over the last few months and they are going to continue mentoring me moving forward. That will help me a lot, their advice is really invaluable for all aspects of my business development. Also, we had a chance to do a fashion show in Ottawa, as part of the original Final, so that was the first time when I've been to Ottawa and it got me some exposure in that market. And of course, the fashion show at Toronto Fashion Week that was sponsored by Mercedes – that was a fantastic opportunity that I wouldn't have had, if it wasn't for the Mercedes Benz Start Up Program.

All of that has brought a lot of attention to my brand and helped raise my profile, generated lots of press, and now more and more people want the product. That is really the bottom line – it's helping me with the sales, which is fantastic.

Victoria West: Where do you retail, besides Gotstyle?

Christopher Bates: In Toronto it's Gotstyle, in Waterloo I'm at Channer's, and in Quebec City I'm at Boutique Novo.

Victoria West: Do you intend to show your collections at Toronto Fashion Week in the future?

Christopher Bates: I do. I'm working on a plan to potentially show in this spring, I would like to. I think it's a great platform, it gets a lot of attention, a lot of press; and I also just really enjoy it. I want to share my work with as many people as possible and that's the best stage in Canada.

Victoria West: Do you know if you're going to do that at the next Toronto Fashion Week yet?

Christopher Bates: I don't know yet. It can be a very costly endeavor, I would want to use the main stage, it has to make sense for my business, and it's really a marketing exercise ultimately. Do I have that much to put into my marketing budget at that time? I don't know yet. But I'd like to find a way to do it.

Victoria West: Where do you find your inspiration?

Christopher Bates: Just life, just living life. I'm really into lots of different things – I love automotive, I love homewares, I love graphic design and typography, I'm into architecture, movies, music. And traveling of course, it's really big. By just living my life, I find certain things that really inspire me and start to generate ideas in my head for clothing – that's sort of how my mind works.

Victoria West: Do you work on any projects right now?

Christopher Bates: Yes, I do. Right now, I'm working on potentially an order for 600 dress shirts, which is really exciting. I'm also shooting my lookbook this week, which will be my Spring 2013 catalogue that I'll be using to then start to pitch more stores on picking up my line for Spring 2013, so I'll be doing a little sales push. I'm also working on a presentation version of my business plan, so I'm going to be meeting with investors. Once that's complete, I'll have to raise financing and invest to grow the business. I'm also working on my new collection for next fall. Right now, it's just in the gestation period, I'm working on the designs, but I've got to get started pretty soon, in order to be on time for the season. So, I'm very busy.

Victoria West: Fashion collaborations between designers and ready-to-wear brands occur more and more frequently these days. The best example would be H&M. Another example would be Martin Lim, the designers who won Mercedes Benz Start Up Program in 2011, and who just launched a capsule collection in collaboration with Reitmans. Would that be a project of interest for you in the future, would you consider doing such collaborative collections with other fashion houses and brands?

59

Christopher Bates: I would for sure, it's actually something that I'm actively pursuing right now. It has to make sense, it should be a brand that I'd like to be affiliated with, and who would like to be affiliated with me, there has to be a good fit.

Victoria West: Do you have any name(s) in mind?

Christopher Bates: I think it would be premature to say that at this point. There are lots of people I'd like to work with on such a project, but I don't want to put anybody out by choosing one category. I'd like to do shoes/footwear – this is something that I'm really keen on at the moment, because I think there is a void in the marketplace for contemporary men's dress shoe. I recently was shopping, I wanted a basic men's contemporary dress shoe in black, and one in brown. I went to just about every shoe place in downtown Toronto, and there are virtually no options. So I have some ideas for what should be out there for men's dress shoes, and I want to help design them and make them. Footwear is probably the first thing that I am keen on; but also I've designed some eyewear, I've also designed homewares. I never really stop designing, so I do want to collaborate, not just with other ready-to-wear clothing manufactures, but also with accessories.

Victoria West: And on a personal note, what is your favorite movie (or movies)?

Christopher Bates: Ah, that's a great one! "Blade Runner", "The Last of the Mohicans" and "The Count of Monte Cristo" are three of my favorites. What I like about these movies is the music, the cinematography, the acting, the directing, and the story – those are the important parts.

Victoria West: What is your favorite movie from the costume perspective?

Christopher Bates: The new "Tron" is a good example – I really liked the costumes, very futuristic and modern and cool; visually, that was a really strong movie.

Another Interview with Canadian Designer Christopher Bates

My second interview with Canadian fashion designer Christopher Bates took place in April 2013, shortly after his showing his new fall collection at World MasterCard Toronto Fashion Week in March 2013. We talked about his new participation at the Fashion Week, about his new collection, and about the next moves that he was about to take in his fashion career.

***

Victoria West: You just showed your fall collection at World MasterCard Toronto Fashion Week, did you meet the expectations that you had for this season's Fashion Week?

Christopher Bates: Absolutely, it was a great experience. The show was well received, there have been lots of great reviews and some new customers.

Victoria West: When your new collection is going to be available in stores?

Christopher Bates: First delivery will be in late August, in the same stores as before – both locations of Gotstyle in Toronto (Bathurst and Distillery District) and Channer's in Waterloo.

Victoria West: What does it take to a Canadian fashion designer to show at Toronto Fashion Week, what are the steps to be taken, from the registration till the actual show on the runway?

Christopher Bates: If you haven't shown before, then you have to apply. It's a fairly detailed application process, you have to submit everything – lookbooks, line sheets, detailed information on your past, your plans, your stores. Then you have to send samples, which will be reviewed. I have already shown before, so for me it was just a matter of expressing my interest in doing a show and paying the fees.

Victoria West: How do you acquire your models for the shows?

Christopher Bates: I have worked with a lot of guys here over the years. I contact agencies and book models. Also, a lot of the guys are my friends and I ask them if they want to do it – they don't do it for free necessarily, but it's great, it really helps me.

Victoria West: Have you started working on your next spring collection yet?

Christopher Bates: Yes, absolutely. I haven't started making the prototypes yet, but I've started with the design process, and I'm going to start making the prototypes very soon.

Victoria West: Besides your spring collection, do you work on any other projects right now?

Christopher Bates: I work on many-many other projects. I'm doing some consulting design for another large fashion brand right now, I can't say what it is, but it's taking all my time at the moment. I'm also doing a couple of homeware projects – pillows, carpets, things like that. I'm also doing a lot of custom work – custom suits, raincoats, dress shirts, this business is really booming right now. I also dress a lot of celebrities for Juno Awards. So yes, my schedule is pretty full right now.

Victoria West: Can we expect to see you at Toronto Fashion Week again?

Christopher Bates: Yes, for sure. Next season I'll be showing either in Toronto, or in Montreal, or both – this would be the plan.

Victoria West: Do you read fashion magazines?

Christopher Bates: Yes, I do. There is a number of magazines for men or for both men and women, and I read both – men's, women's, unisex.

Victoria West: What are your favorites?

Christopher Bates: I like "Fashion", the men's and the women's version; "Dress to Kill"; "Product"; "Flare", which is a classic; "Sharp". There is also "Women's Wear Daily" that I like, which is more of a newspaper type of publication, but overall this is really my favorite source for fashion news.

Victoria West: How do you like to spend your free time?

Christopher Bates: I go to the gym or play soccer, I do sports 7 days a week, that's really important to me, I love being healthy. It's a stress reliever as well, I feel so much better after exercising. I listen to music, I read books, I cook, I host a lot of dinner parties, I like spending time with friends and family, I love to travel, I love movies.

An Interview with Adam Bledin, Creative Director of Lazypants

Lazypants is a Canadian brand of casual clothing, with the operative word "lazy", meaning "comfortable". Adam Bledin is the Creative Director of Lazypants, and I met him in November 2012 during a fashion event in Toronto when he showcased the newest Lazypants collection. That particular collection featured Lazypants sweatpants, skinnies and hoodies in 18 vibrant colors. I had a chat with Adam Bledin during that night, and this is what he shared about what it is to be lazy.

***

Victoria West: Please tell us a bit about yourself and about Lazypants.

Adam Bledin: I'm the Creative Director of Rebus, which makes Lazypants. Lazypants is a type of sweatpants, and the whole idea behind it is to be comfortable. The question we keep asking everybody is: "What is your lazy?" When you say "lazy", it doesn't mean sitting at home doing nothing, it could be riding a bike, it could be reading a newspaper, it doesn't matter, it's your time off from the world. What is your lazy? That's what Lazypants are all about – comfortable when you're doing your lazy.

Victoria West: Please tell us more about tonight's event.

Adam Bledin: The event is a TNT party in Yorkville. We offer a discount of 20% off anything Lazypant material, and $10 of each will go to Ovarian Cancer Research, a charity I fully support.

Victoria West: When a shopper comes to Lazypants, what will they find?

Adam Bledin: They'll find 18 different colors, and comfort, and style.

Victoria West: And except lazy pants, what else?

Adam Bledin: Except lazy pants we also offer lazy hoodies and skinny lazies.

Victoria West: Where do you retail?

Adam Bledin: We retail in Toronto at TNT, Holt Renfrew, Sporting Life. As to other cities, we're all over Canada – Vancouver, Montreal; but also in New York and Los Angeles.
Victoria West: Who is your target shopper?

Adam Bledin: People who like to be comfortable, people who like to be lazy.

An Interview with Canadian Actress Tonya Lee Williams, Founder of ReelWorld Film Festival

ReelWorld Film Festival (or RWFF) was founded by Canadian actress Tonya Lee Williams in 2001, and it's taken place in Toronto each year ever since. It's a festival dedicated to diversity, and the artists and film makers who showcase their films at ReelWorld come from all ethnicity backgrounds from all other the world. I first attended ReelWorld Film Festival in 2012, and this was the year when I also met Tonya Lee Williams for the fist time.

The festival takes place each year in April, but before that, in March every ear, the Founders and the Board of Directors of RWFF invite media from Toronto to a press conference to announce the upcoming festival's events that would take place the following month. During the annual ReelWorld Film Festival 2013 press conference I had the opportunity to interview Tonya Lee Williams, the Founder and Executive Director of the festival, and to talk about RWFF 2013 which was about to showcase more than 80 films from 17 different countries, among them feature films, documentaries and music videos.

***

Victoria West: Looking back at 2001 when you founded ReelWorld Film Festival, do you think you achieved what you were hoping for, after these 13 years, or even more than you hoped for?

Tonya Lee Williams: I don't know, not more that I hoped for, but exactly what I actually thought. We needed a place, a meeting place, let's say an oasis, where all these diverse film makers could come together, share their experiences, and help each other. What I've watched over the 13 years is how they have bonded. They are now working together, they have produced and directed films, built production companies, and that's really what I wanted the festival to be – it's the oasis where we come together, and share, and move forward. It was also a great platform to attract a lot of distributors and more senior professionals in the industry to be able to impart their knowledge to a lot of these emerging artists.

At the time when we started the festival, there was really nothing like it. There wasn't a place where people could just go every year: "This is where I can put my film, this is where I can meet people who can help my career". The fact that that keeps happening, is what my expectation always was; and if that keeps happening, then this is where I meant it to be.

Victoria West: What are you the most excited for about this year's ReelWorld Film Festival?

Tonya Lee Williams: I think the programming is so superior this year. We have some amazing films. Not only do we have 66% Canadian films this year, but we also show films from Egypt, Iran, Uganda, Nigeria, UK, Ireland, Caribbean, Guadalupe. We have the first film from a female director from Guadalupe at the festival this year. The films are absolutely amazing. I'm also very proud of our music video program. When people think music videos, I think they are always thinking hip-hop and urban music; but it's an art form, and there are so many directors doing so many beautiful things, visually beautiful things, and that's what we want people to look at when they look at the music videos that we programmed this year.

Also, industry series – people forget that a film festival is not just screening films. We have amazing panels. Telefilm is doing a panel that is the best panel for people who are emerging film makers and who are always saying: "How do I get my film made, how do I get financing, how do I move it to the next step?" This is the panel you need to be at. Another wonderful panel is the panel with The Writers' Guild of Canada – there is a lot of writers who want to get into TV shows; how do you become a part of a writers' team? This panel is about that.

And then the networking events that we do – when we say networking, we think less about parties, we don't think much networking thing happens at parties. We do a brunch with an Ontario Media Development Corporation support session where people can talk and sit, and be casual and comfortable, and yet in a working environment.

Another event we do is Face2Face, which is an opportunity for emerging artists to have 15 minutes one-on-one time with more senior professionals to talk about whether they are pitching a project or if they are trying to move their careers to the next level.

So there are so many components! What's great is we have an amazing website that Wired Messenger developed, and we just launched it on March 20th. On the website, there is everything – an opportunity for people to see information about more that 84 films that are in the festival this year, and to see all the different workshops, and panels, and everything that's going on, including our Reel Youth screening, which happens on Wednesday, Thursday and Friday (April 12th, 13th,

14th). Schools bring kids age 8 to 13 to see an amazing production of some films that we've gotten from the National Film Board, and also LIFT is doing a workshop for them. So there is a lot in 5 days.

Victoria West: How it is decided which films to be screened for the opening and closing nights?

Tonya Lee Williams: We do it as a collective. I worked with 7 programmers this year (I was the director of programming), and we looked at everything. This year we're opening with a film from Ghana, "Contract"; in fact, there are not many films that have come from Ghana. Every year we try to look for what's the community that we should spotlight a bit this year. That film is a hilarious one, a comedy. We're closing with a salvation Bollywood film, "Aayna Ka Bayna", but a Bollywood film with a twist that has a modern take on how Bollywood films are done.

These are done as a collective. We as programmers get together, we discuss all the programming, we look at what we think is the strongest film to open the festival with, what would be to close the festival, and then what pieces to put all in the centre.

Victoria West: How do you see ReelWorld Film Festival in the future, let's say in 10 years from now?

Tonya Lee Williams: Ten years from now? I want it to be the same festival actually. I just want a bigger audience. I want the Canadian audience to come to the festival excited to see what Canadian artists are doing, what international emerging artists are doing, so for me the growth at this point is always about the audience. We have great filmmakers, we have great films, we have incredible staff, we have phenomenal programmers – that is all great. If I can keep all that up, then I am really happy. What I still find challenging is how to get the audience to get out of their bed, get in their car and come down to Canada Square and check out the five days of the festival. And I think most film festivals struggle with this, but it's something that we work on all the time. TIFF, Cannes – everybody struggles with it. But I think that's what I would want in 10 years – everything to be sold out, every single film.

And we have to expand the festival. Sometimes people even now say to me: "The festival is 5 days, why don' you make it longer?" I said I would not make the festival longer, until I see every film is filled in the five days. Then I will know it's time to expand it. But there is no point to make the festival longer for no reason.

Short Films Featured at ReelWorld Film Festival 2013 in Toronto

One of the films showcased at ReelWorld Film Festival 2013 was the Canadian short drama "Eneme" directed by Chris Abell. After the recent death of his son, Boyd (played by actor Edsson Morales) is deciding between his own life and death. Canadian Features Programmer Bobby Del Rio said: "Edsson Morales delivers a powerhouse performance in this well-crafted short film about one man's pain".

During the annual press conference from March 2013 preceding ReelWorld Film Festival of the same year I had the opportunity to chat with the filmmakers of the short drama "Eneme" – director Chris Abell, producers Brendan Whelton and Chris Green, lead actor Edsson Morales.

When I asked the four of them to tell me about the making of the film, Chris Abell told me that Edsson Morales had come to him with an idea, they collaborated on the script, and then, over a couple of months, they brought over producers Chris Green and Brendan Whelton. After that, the idea just flew through Edsson's style of acting and Chris's style of directing. Chris Abell and Edsson Morales tried to create a very dark atmosphere inside the characters. The location was brought to them by the producers coming on board, and within three months the film was shot. The editing of the film took approximately another three months. This is the first festival the short film "Eneme" would have been showcased at.

Producers Brendan Whelton and Chris Green shared that for them the making of this film was a really great experience. Brendan Whelton was approached by actor Edsson Morales, and since the two producers have worked with Edsson on a feature film in the past, they were looking forward to working with him on a new film again, so they decided to come on board of "Eneme". They had gone through 8-9 drafts of the script until it was locked. Once the script was decided upon, the shooting started and everything came together really quickly. As the film developed, Brendan said, the producers passed the ball to Chris Abell and Edsson Morales – they just needed to make sure that they stayed out of the director and lead actor's way and let them get where they needed to go. Brendan Whelton and Chris Green even joked that there was a very cold weekend when they shot the film, but it was an awesome experience for them.

Then I asked Edsson Morales to share about his experience with the film. He told me that from an actor's point of view, it was an amazing project to work on, thanks to the team that the film had and thanks to Chris Abell, the director. "It was awesome to work with him [Chris Abell]. Whenever you needed someone to help you dig and get into that moment, or get into that character, Chris [Abell] was definitely there. Also, our producers Brendan Whelton and Chris Green made it an easier environment to work in. It was really great how they pulled it together. For me as an actor, it was an awesome script to work with. Also, my co-star Leo [was great] – he's 10 years old, he is a very talented young man, and it was awesome to work with him. And yes, it was definitely a very cold weather when we shot the film, but it was an amazing experience."

Director Chris Abell shared that he hoped this film to be a reflection. "Eneme" reflects the idea of a man who's lost his son. How someone in this situation would feel, what would they be forced to go through, and what would they do about it? Taking it to the extremes? What Chris hoped for is that the audience would feel the heartache and the pain of the lead character and reflect on it.

***

Young Emerging Actors Assembly (YEAA) and ACTRA Toronto featured nine short films coming from experienced and emerging Canadian artists during ReelWorld Film Festival 2013. The nine short films were "Bejide", "A Man Is a Man Is a Man", "To Hell with Love", "The Change", "The Haircut", "The New Domain", "Audition Day", "The Sound That Broke the Silence" and "Getaway Car".

During the same press conference for ReelWorld Film Festival 2013 I also interviewed another group of emerging artists, the film makers of three out of nine short films mentioned above – Clara Pasieka, Raven Dauda and Richard Young. Clara Pasieka is the writer, executive producer and actress in the short film "Bejide", but she also had a role in the film "Audition Day". Raven Dauda is the other actress in the film "Bejide". Richard Young is the filmmaker of the short film "Audition Day", but he also acted in "A Man Is a Man Is a Man" and "Getaway Car".

The film "Bejide" was the first screen play for Clara Pasieka. She is not only an actress, but also a playwright. It was her first time as a filmmaker and she shared that she was really excited about that. But as an actor, she had done a lot of work in theater, film and television.

For Clara, ReelWorld Film Festival is a platform to tell stories that are important to her. She thinks it can be really difficult to find a place where people can hear the stories that emerging filmmakers want to tell – that's the tricky thing for young filmmakers, to find a festival that would be interested in hearing those stories. Clara has always been interested in writing multicultural plays and screenplays for theater and film. This is a really unique festival, she said, and to her it's an absolute honor to tell stories that reflect the diversity and multiculturality showcased by this festival.

Raven Dauda has been an actor in Canada for over 20 years. She said that she loved film festivals. She has been a part of Toronto International Film Festival, as well as a part of Sundance Festival; and now, being a part of ReelWorld Film Festival was a real honor for her and she admitted she was very excited about it.

Raven thinks that as an actor, primarily in this festival, it's just wonderful to have this type of support. Canada has a rich pool of talent, so for her being a part of a festival like this helps showcase that, helps showcase the sense of diversity, and allows Canadians to know exactly what our country's artists have to say.

For Richard Young the main scope of this partnership between YEAA and ReelWorld Film Festival is to give the emerging artists and filmmakers the necessary space to create films and work on them together. All these short films were made by ACTRA members or actors. Richard thinks that in this country Canadian actors need to be true artists and take the reigns of their own career. They cannot wait around for the agent to call them, they need to find a way to create their own works. In this collective of short films Richard and his partners have worked with people who are first time filmmakers. The films are great, but there is a learning process of being an actor, a producer, a writer, and taking back the control of their own career, by saying: "Here's my voice, I can do it, it's not as difficult as I thought it was going to be, and I have something to say". Richard thinks that ReelWorld Film Festival provides that support by giving a voice to the people who want to share their stories.

When I asked the three artists what do they think about the future of the short film in Canada, Clara Pasieka told me that in her opinion the short films are the building blocks for many of filmmakers into creating bigger stories and feature films. But she also thinks that this country needs to pay more attention to short films, because there are a lot of amazing short films in Canada that people don't see, because they don't know about them. She said: "We need to start getting Canada watching short films, and we need to do that by featuring short films on television. I think filmmakers are taking some incredible risks and they are telling some incredible stories that they wouldn't necessarily be able to or have the option to tell these stories in feature long films. So it's really important we get Canada watch short films – I'm astounded when I see all these amazing Canadian short films from so many talented artists."

An interview with Canadian actor Clé Bennett

And last but not least in this book section, I would like to introduce you to Canadian actor Clé Bennett, whom I had the opportunity to interview in September 2013. He has acted in film, television and theatre; he is known to the public from such films and TV shows like "Barney's Version", "Rookie Blue", "Murdoch Mysteries", "The Line", "Cracked", "Guns", "Lost Girl", "The Listener", "Republic of Doyle", "The Line" and other productions. He worked along Paul Giamatti and Dustin Hoffmann in the film "Barney's Version". During this interview we talked about his acting career from past and present, about his films, about his roles and characters, about his plans for the future.

***

Victoria West: How and when did you decide to become an actor?

Clé Bennett: I have always been an actor, even before I knew what it was called. From when I was a child, the one thing I was most passionate about was portraying different characters or playing make-believe. "Acting" is just the professional term for playing make-believe. I didn't decide to become an actor – I simply embraced the fact that I am an actor, and then acted on it.

Victoria West: When was the first time you worked as a professional actor? Please tell us more about that production.

Clé Bennett: My first project was a short film called "Shudder", directed by Brett Sullivan, who I had the pleasure of reuniting with on "Flashpoint". I remember being super excited, and maybe just a little too eager to prove myself (laughs). Overall, I remember feeling very comfortable on set. I knew it was where I was meant to be, and I intended to stay for a long time to come.

Victoria West: You've worked as an actor for TV, film and theatre – which of them do you love the most and why?

Clé Bennett: I enjoy acting in every medium, but I'd have to say I prefer acting on camera, whether that's TV or film. I appreciate the challenge, and exhilaration of live performance that the stage provides, but I love rising to the challenge of portraying the realistic human subtlety that the camera demands.

Victoria West: When you act, how easy or difficult is it for you to transport yourself into your character's skin and shoes?

Clé Bennett: It kind of depends on the role, but I've had a lot of practice becoming different characters from when I was a little kid playing make-believe. I focus on "becoming" the character, instead of "acting" like the character. Sometimes the more a character differs from me, the easier it is to play.

Victoria West: Do you find you have a lot in common, or anything at all, with your characters?

Clé Bennett: Again, it depends on the character. But I actually make a point of not injecting myself into my characters. The whole point of acting is to become somebody else.

Victoria West: Who is your favorite character you've played so far and why?

Clé Bennett: I loved playing Carlos in "The Line". Carlos was a complex, multidimensional character, with big problems. Definitely my favorite kind of character to play.

Victoria West: You currently appear as Officer Wesley Cole in ABC's "Rookie Blue", please tell us more about this project and your role.

Clé Bennett: Wes shows up at the hospital after Chloe gets shot, and he reveals to Dov that he's Chloe's husband. Wes and Chloe were former partners in another precinct, and one weekend after a string of back-to-back shifts they took off to Niagara to party, and ended up tying the knot just for kicks. Soon after, Chloe was transferred and they lost contact, but the reality is Wes has strong feelings for Chloe that he's always kept to himself. Now with her life on the line, he regrets his silence, and believes this may be his second chance with her. Problem is, she's kind of in a relationship with Dov at the moment! What happens next ought to be interesting!

Victoria West: What's in the cards for you in the near future?

Clé Bennett: I'm currently working on some new projects, and have a few others on the horizon that I'm unable to mention just yet. But in the short term, look for me to appear as Xavier Reed a.k.a. "The Mayor" on Season 2 of The CW's "Arrow"; as

Wes Cole in Season 5 of ABC's "Rookie Blue"; and as the voice of 2-Bit in the animated series "Mother Up".

Victoria West: Can you tell us what are the accomplishment(s) you dream to achieve in your acting career?

Clé Bennett: I'm not gonna say, but you'll definitely find out after I achieve them!

Victoria West: Do you have a role model, an artist to be your inspiration, your mentor, whom you look up to?

Clé Bennett: I don't really have any particular role models or mentors, however I'm inspired by many different artists.

Victoria West: And on a personal note, how do you like to spend your free time?

Clé Bennett: Free time? What's that? (Laughs.)

***

RE: Last answer – case in point. Now that I think of it, I have given the same answer to this question more than once.

Part III

BOOK REVIEWS

"Sex and the City" by Candace Bushnell

One of the best-selling authors that are ever present in my personal library is Candace Bushnell. I'm a passionate reader, and I go to my favorite bookstore from Toronto every now and again to indulge in some great reads. I have acquired and read all the books by Candace Bushnell that I could lay my hands on – "Sex and the City", "Four Blondes", "Trading Up", "Lipstick Jungle", "One Fifth Avenue", "The Carrie Diaries" and "Summer and the City".

The first book by Candace Bushnell I have ever read was "Sex and the City". Before becoming a book, then an overly popular TV show, then two acclaimed movies, "Sex and the City" was a column written by Candace Bushnell in the "New York Observer" newspaper, just like Carrie Bradshaw's column in the "New York Star" fictional newspaper in the TV show which aired in 1998-2004 was. If you go to the "New York Observer" online archive, you can still see some of the original column articles written by Candace Bushnell back in the nineties. When I browsed the archive, I actually recognized some of those articles from "Sex and the City" the book. Candace Bushnell used to write her column about her and her friends' dating experiences in the city of New York, which was the basic inspiration for "Sex and the City" the TV show, and which inspired the television characters Carrie Bradshaw, Miranda Hobbes, Samantha Jones and Charlotte York.

"Sex and the City" is a hilarious and a very honest book, just like the other books written by this author are. What I like the most about Candace Bushnell's books is their sincerity. The author is not afraid to call a spade a spade, and she calls things by their names. The way sex life of people in New York is dissected in this book is sharp and outrageous. Bushnell discusses every single aspect of one's sex life with a great deal of honesty, which makes this book so hilarious. The "fuck" word is commonly used in Candace Bushnell's books and it should come as no surprise. If people in New York and elsewhere use this word on a common basis (although more sensible people, like Charlotte York, prefer the less disturbing "the F word" expression), why wouldn't this word appear in the same way in a book about people in New York?

The book was ultimately the inspiration for the first season of the TV show, with characters and situations from the book which were adapted to the show, although there are many differences between the two as well. Carrie Bradshaw, Miranda Hobbes, Samantha Jones and Charlotte York from the book are totally different from those in the TV show. The closest resemblance is in Carrie's case, who is a columnist both in the book and in the show. Meanwhile, Miranda is a cable executive in the book, but a lawyer in the series; Samantha is a movie producer in the book, but a PR manager in the TV series; Charlotte is an English journalist in the book, but an American WASP in the TV show. Also, the television series stresses out the friendship of the four women more than the book does.

The show begins almost the same way as the book – an English journalist comes to New York, meets an eligible bachelor, dates him for several weeks, sees a house with him, and then never hears from him again. But in the book, as opposed to the show, Charlotte York is the English journalist left out by the lying bachelor.

There are also other characters from the book translated into the series, and some of them are adapted differently as well. There is Skipper Johnson, a guy who just hangs out in the book, but who is one of Miranda's boyfriends in the show. The gay Stanford Blatch, screen writer in the book, talent agent in the show. Barkley, the modelizer. The Bone, the beautiful male model. Amalita Amalfi, the international prostitute. Mr. Marvelous, one of Mr. Big's friends. And of course, Mr. Big himself.

Quite a few stories from the book are translated into the first season of the TV show. There is the relationship between Carrie and Big. There is the story of the women who have sex like men. There is the story about modelizers. There is the story about the so-called "high-class" hookers, who call themselves "international girlfriends" – women who don't want to work and seek rich men who would pay for their rent. There is the Secret Sex story. There is the Threesome story. There is the story of Stanford Blatch "proposing" to a straight woman for a convenient social life. There is the Baby Shower story. And last but not least, the story of Carrie and Big's relationship and their break up.

"Four Blondes" by Candace Bushnell

The second book by Candace Bushnell, after "Sex and the City", is "Four Blondes", published in 2000. As the title suggests, it's a book about four blonde women, and each of them has her own story – the book is a 4-in-1 story. The four blondes are the model Janey Wilcox, the columnist Winney Deeke, the socialite Cecelia Kelly Luxenstein and the writer Minky.

Janey Wilcox is a girl who would do anything to get what she wants. When her story starts in "Four Blondes", she is not in the greatest place. She has no money, but she wants a lavish lifestyle, and she is constantly looking for a man who would pay for that. She wants to spend every summer in Hamptons, but she cannot afford it by herself, so she starts a "relationship" with a rich man she would spend the summer in Hamptons with. By the end of the summer, any of her Hamptons "relationships" would end with no doubt. As long as she doesn't expect all these men to marry her, she will always have a good summer in Hamptons, and she is willing to put up with men's humiliations in order to get a summer house in Hamptons. Every time she is asked about it, she says that she just wants a good summer. There was Peter, there was Zack Manners, there was Harold, there was Redmon Richardly, there was Comstock Dibble. None of these "relationships" were fulfilling for Janey of course, but she doesn't care, as long as she gets what she wants. It's just sex and summer in Hamptons. At a certain point she wonders why rich people won't do more for girls like her, for that amount of money would mean nothing to them. But then, as she realizes herself, rich people don't like to be used. Of course they don't like it. Who on earth would like to be taken advantage of, rich or poor?

People think of Janey Wilcox as a slut, or even worse, as a whore; but again, she doesn't care, as long as she gets what she wants. She is convinced that someday she will meet the perfect man she would fall madly in love with, and marry him.

Her own mother is not like any other normal mothers. She is not loving, she is not understanding, she is not supporting. Janey and her mother hate each other. So Janey is determined "to show" her mother (and everybody else who gives her a hard time) that she can do much better in her life than her unsupporting and unloving mother has ever been able to do. Janey thinks her mother is just frustrated and jealous. The only thing her mother ever says to Janey is that she should take care of her beauty and her weight in order to get a rich man and marry him, otherwise she's doomed. Her mother thinks Janey shouldn't work, she thinks that beautiful women don't have to work, that beautiful women should find themselves rich men to provide for them. She keeps bugging Janey about marriage. No wonder the two of them don't get along that well.

And then Comstock Dibble, the movie producer, comes along, who is another of her summer "relationships". He gives her $20,000 to rent her own summer house in Hamptons. This time, Janey is determined "to do something with her life", so she attempts to write a screenplay for Comstock Dibble. Whether she finishes it or not, that's another issue. But of course, Comstock Dibble is not different from any other men Janey Wilcox has met. He only has anal sex with her, so she won't get pregnant. And at the end of the summer, he introduces her to his fiancée, and admits they actually try to get pregnant.

In the end, things get better for Janey, and she actually manages to do all that by herself, without a rich man attached. She gets a two-million dollar contract from Victoria's Secret for four years, and a nice new Porsche Boxster convertible. Not bad for a single woman, she thinks.

***

The next story from "Four Blondes" is the story of Winnie and James Deeke, both journalists. A fake marriage. They have nothing in common, they don't understand each other, they even doubt they love each other anymore. They are very competitive. They can't talk to each other about their marital issues (or about any issues, for that matter), because their marriage is lacking any sort of communication whatsoever. Sometimes they feel about each other like they are two strangers. Their marriage is nothing else but a social bargain. Why on earth would two people marry just for the social convenience's sake? It's not for a foreseeable future like a business, it's for a lifetime. How are you going to live with a man happily ever after, if the only reason you married him (and took his name) is you expected to become the wife of a famous writer? And if he doesn't become a famous writer, then what?

***

Meet Cecelia Kelly Luxenstein, the socialite, and her husband Hubert Luxenstein, the European prince. Yet another fake marriage. Yet another social bargain. Nothing special, nothing romantic, nothing lovely is going on between Prince and Princess Luxenstein. And because of that, Cecelia is depressed, anorexic, almost addicted to drugs, incapable of bringing herself together, intolerant to fame and Page Six (God knows nobody would like the kind of Page Six fame), seeing a shrink who seems unable to help her.

The funniest scene in this story is the scene when right after their marriage, Cecelia asks for money from her husband to buy new clothes, and her husband makes his point to tell her that she's got a full closet of clothes, and that marrying him has never meant receiving money for clothes.

Although they have been together for four years and married for two, Princess Cecelia realizes they have nothing in common, she knows nothing about her husband, they act like two strangers, they always fight, they are literally from Mars and Venus. Why did they get married again?

***

The last Blonde from the book is a writer from New York who realizes there are no eligible men in Manhattan anymore. New York is so rotten, it became impossible to get a decent relationship here. So she flies to London, in search for true love, and maybe a husband. But what she actually discovers is not what she expected to discover at all. Sex and love habits of London people are very different from those of New York people, and not in a good way, not in a way which would make an American woman happy. So she goes back to New York and meets her love on the plane; and then she realizes that the grass is not greener on the other side of Atlantic after all.

"Trading Up" by Candace Bushnell

"Trading Up" is the third novel by Candace Bushnell, after "Sex and the City" and "Four Blondes", published in 2003. It's the sequel to the story about Janey Wilcox from "Four Blondes". She is a celebrity now, a well-known Victoria's Secret model. And yet again, she has to put up with a lot of humiliations from men around, because she is still not taken as seriously as she would like to. Her ultimate purpose in life is to climb socially. She wants to be invited to the most glamorous parties in Manhattan, to befriend the most influential people, to get into the most selected circles, and of course, to find a rich man who would provide for her. So she would do anything to have it all. She befriends the socialite Mimi Kilroy, the queen of the social scene in Manhattan, but their friendship is far from sincere. She manages to get a rich man and become his wife – MovieTime president Selden Rose. Finally, she got a man who would take care of her, at least so to speak. But the two of them have nothing in common. Their marriage is fake and lacking love. Janey admits to herself that a marriage like hers is nothing else but a luxury prostitution. They fight all the time. Rose gets mad every time Janey tries to show other people how smart she is, when in fact he thinks she is utterly stupid.

Fake marriages are commonly present in Candace Bushnell's books, just like insecure women characters who are unable to do anything smart in their life like graduate from a good school or find a decent job, and who want men to pay for their rent. Candace Bushnell is not afraid to put her finger on these specifics of Manhattan behavior. She is very sincere and straightforward about Sugar Daddy's girlfriends and their phony marriages.

Things take a bad turn for Janey when Comstock Dibble reveals the specifics of their past relationship to the press (including the money he had given her), and suddenly Janey becomes the social leper. Tabloid papers, and then everybody else, call her the model prostitute. She tries to bring herself back on track after this social disaster, but to no avail. Selden Rose is blackmailed to divorce her, as "he can't handle women like Janey Wilcox". Once Janey finds out about her husband's perspectives to divorce her, she flies away to Los Angeles to start a new life. And eventually she manages to do just that – she gets her second chance in L.A.

Candace Bushnell's books are sharp and outrageous, so their happy endings don't really sound like a cliché. It wasn't surprising for me that Janey got well in the end. It would have been surprising the other way. Too much is too much, isn't it? After all she has been through, Janey Wilcox finally finds her way, all by herself. She didn't even need a man for that. See, you can do it, baby.

"Lipstick Jungle" by Candace Bushnell

"Lipstick Jungle" is the fourth novel by Candace Bushnell, published in 2005. Sharp, outrageous, pinpointing, sincere, honest, a great page turner – just a few words I would use to describe it, the way I am already used to Candace Bushnell's brilliant writing which made me read all her books one after another, in one single breath. "Lipstick Jungle" is the story of three powerful women in their forties in New York City: Wendy Healy the movie producer, Nico O'Neilly the editor in chief of a fashion magazine, Victory Ford the designer. They are a close threesome, and their friendship is what they cherish the most. While reading the book, I was thinking about the other friendship group created by Candace Bushnell – the "Sex and the City" foursome. The two female groups from "Sex and the City" and "Lipstick Jungle" have a lot in common, but the most important things bonding them are their golden friendship and their steel independence as struggling women in New York City. And, of course, their excellent sense of style and fashion.

The three women are high professionals at the top of their fields, but their personal life is not as happy as they wish it was. Wendy Healy is married with three children, and she became the man in her family, as her husband Shane proved to be untalented at any project he ever started, without accomplishing anything notable, so he just resigned himself to stay at home and take care of the kids. Soon both of them start to resent this situation, which leads to their estrangement which leads to their divorce. But in the end, Wendy is glad to get out of a marriage which doesn't make her happy anymore. She gets her second chance when she starts a relationship with Selden

Rose, one of her colleagues, a relationship which is more fulfilling to her than her 12-year marriage ever was. As to her career, she feels even happier and more fulfilled when the movie she produces, "Ragged Pilgrims", becomes a sound success.

Nico O'Neilly is married as well, and she has a teenage daughter. She is not happy with her husband Seymour neither, after 14 years of marriage. They are not so close anymore, she feels their passion has died away, they don't even have sex anymore. At the beginning, this was frustrating and infuriating for Nico; but as the time passed, and as she got consumed by her work more and more, she just stopped thinking and caring about the lack of sex in their marriage. And then she meets Kirby Atwood, the young aspiring actor, a very handsome man, whom she has a passionate affair with. Suddenly, Nico feels alive again. They keep seeing each other in secret for months, and Nico doesn't even have the courage to admit her relationship with Kirby to her closest friends. But as soon as some rumors about her affair with Kirby start to spread in New York, she stops seeing him without delay. It is a difficult decision for her to make, but the least thing she wants to do is to disappoint her daughter whom she adores. So in the end, she chooses to come back to her family over continuing her passionate affair with Kirby. Meanwhile, she also makes an important up-step in her career, by getting a coveted promotion.

Victory is single with no children, dedicated to her career. Some "thinking in the box" journalists consider her kind of disabled for "not having a family as per the socially demanded standards", but she couldn't care less. She enjoys her career, which is the most important thing in her life. She had her ups and downs, but she always kept going. She starts dating Lyne

Bennett, a billionaire. Some may think that a man like Bennett, consumed by his business and more billions to make, is not able to commit in a profound relationship, but it's not his case. He's sweet, loving and caring, and he really is into Victory. Both of them have volcanic temperaments, which affects their relationship. But in the end, they come to the conclusion that they have quite a lot in common, so they decide to get over their couple issues and remain together.

The end of the book is a happy one for all three of them, as they find a way to reach happiness and fulfillment both in their love lives and in their careers. "Lipstick Jungle" is the world of powerful and independent women, who get on top only due to their hard work, ambition, dedication and commitment.

Once again, Candace Bushnell puts her finger on the poor marital behavior in New York City. Problematic and unhappy marriages are featured in this book as well, just as in the other books by Candace Bushnell. It seems that it's quite difficult to live happily ever after in New York City, as the writer's books suggest. No wonder they say the divorce rate in North America is so high. Somehow, marriage stopped to be a source of happiness for people, as it used to be.

"Lipstick Jungle" was turned into a TV show, starring Brooke Shields as Wendy, Kim Raver as Nico and Lindsay Price as Victory. It aired in 2008-2009 and had two seasons. There are some differences between the book and the TV show (as it always happens), but it follows the main plot of the book, at least in the first season.

"One Fifth Avenue" by Candace Bushnell

A really incisive book from Candace Bushnell is "One Fifth Avenue", published in 2008. It's a story about One Fifth Avenue address in New York and its glamorous (or not so) tenants. Fifth Avenue is THE street in Manhattan – the street of rich, the street of powerful, the street of those who are on top. And One Fifth Avenue is THE address – the most coveted, the most craved, the most desired, the chicest, the hottest, the one with the best pedigree, the one with all the most interesting people. If you live at One Fifth Avenue, you really made it.

The intrigues at One Fifth Avenue are tangled by its tenants themselves. Philip Oakland, a writer. Enid Merle, his aunt, a gossip columnist. Schiffer Diamond, a Hollywood actress. James and Mindy Gooch, a writer and a journalist. Annalisa and Paul Rice, a lawyer and a businessman. And of course, Lola Fabrikant, the One Fifth Avenue tenant wannabe.

Once Mrs. Houghton, the old social queen of New York, is dead, the battle for her penthouse apartment at One Fifth Avenue is on. It's won by the Rice couple, rich people from Washington. And once they move in, the conflict between the building tenants is going to be tenser than ever. Everybody is craving for Mrs. Houghton's luxurious penthouse apartment from One Fifth Avenue, but not everybody can actually afford it, hence the tensions between the building tenants. Mindy Gooch is the one to suffer the most from the tenant changes in the building, because she is frustrated by living in the best building in the city, but occupying the worst apartment in it, an apartment on the main floor which used to be a storage space before it was upgraded to a living apartment. So she constantly badgers her husband James about their living conditions; about buying a better apartment in the building which they can't actually afford because they are just a middle class couple; about his books which aren't really on the bestselling list; about their marriage which is far from perfect as well, and so on and so forth.

Another hilarious character, so Candace Bushnell-esque, is Lola Fabrikant, the One Fifth Avenue tenant wannabe, and Philip Oakland's girlfriend wannabe as well. Lola, a young but ambitious girl, comes to New York "to make her life". She manages to get hired by Philip Oakland, and soon after that she also manages to seduce him, calling herself his girlfriend. If it seems to you that she's a stupid girl, don't be fooled. She may not know any serious things about life, she may not know what hard and honest work means, she may not have ever tried to do something notable in her life by herself, but she knows perfectly what she wants, and she always finds a way to get it. And what does she want? Nothing special – just a nice little place like One Fifth Avenue to live at, and a nice man like Philip Oakland to pay for her expenses. Things are going according to her plan for a while, while Philip is caught in this relationship "by default". But once Phillip detangles himself from Lola and gets engaged to love of his life Schiffer Diamond, Lola quickly finds another man to pay her bills – James Gooch, who suddenly does become a best-selling writer and gets rich overnight. Lola Fabrikant is one of Candace Bushnell's characters often met in her books – women who don't want to move a finger to do anything decent in their lives, but who want to fool some rich man to provide for them.

Fake marriages are also present in this book, just like in other books by Candace Bushnell. It's surprising how two people who have nothing in common get married and manage to live together for years, just to get to a point when they practically hate each other. One of these couples are Mindy and James Gooch. Although they have had a long marriage, although they have a teenage boy, they act like total strangers. More than that – they hate each other. Mindy hates her husband for not being a successful writer, for not being a multi-millionaire, and for not being able to afford a more expensive apartment in their building; while James hates Mindy for not being a supportive wife and for always underestimating and undermining him.

Another fake marriage is that of Annalisa and Paul Rice's. They are the rich couple who manage to snatch the coveted penthouse apartment from One Fifth; but what they can't manage to do is to get beyond their money and their banking accounts. Their marriage goes from fake to dangerous; thoughts of killing spouse cross their minds; and so, Annalisa finds a way to get rid of her husband who started to step on her toes.

Once again, Candace Bushnell serves us a sharp and outrageous book about New York people and their social habits. One of these habits is that everyone is a writer, or a writer wannabe. Philip Oakland and James Gooch are, of course, credited writers. But there are lots of other writers in this book. Enid Merle, Philip's aunt, is a gossip columnist. Mindi Gooch works in Publishing and writes a blog about her frustrating life. Thayer, a friend of Lola's, is a blogger who writes a very popular blog about social events and people from New York. Even Lola Fabrikant fancies herself as a writer at some point and starts writing a sex column on a blog. An inflation of writers in New York City.

And "One Fifth Avenue" is not the only book by Candace Bushnell abounding with writers or writer wannabes. First of all, her consecrated character Carrie Bradshaw from "Sex and the City" and "The Carrie Diaries" is a writer. Then Janey Wilcox from "Four Blondes" and "Trading Up" comes along, attempting "to be a writer" and trying to write a movie script. Whether she finishes it or not, that's a different story. Then the other blondes from "Four Blondes" write as well – the journalist Winnie Deeke and the writer Minky. Lots and lots of writers in Candace Bushnell's books, literally an invasion of writers. Some of them are real writers all right, like Carrie Bradshaw of Philip Oakland for instance, but how about the others? While reading Candace Bushnell's books, I couldn't help but wonder (the brilliant Carrie Bradshaw's famous quote) – does everybody in New York aspire to be a writer?

"The Carrie Diaries" by Candace Bushnell

"The Carrie Diaries", the sixth novel by Candace Bushnell, is the story of Carrie Bradshaw before "Sex and the City". The book focuses on Carrie Bradshaw's senior year of high school in a small town called Castlebury. As we read the book, we meet Carrie's family, her friends, her mates from the high school. Then we meet Sebastian Kydd, the new guy from the high school who becomes the most popular guy overnight, the guy wanted by all the girls, the guy Carrie falls in love with instantly. Then she starts going out with him, but is utterly disappointed when she discovers that her best friend Lali steals him from her. Then she gets accepted to Brown college.

However, "The Carrie Diaries" is not only the story of Carrie's senior year of high school, but it's also Carrie's story of becoming a writer. Being a writer is her most cherished dream, and she feels ready to make her way toward a writing career. She applies for a summer writing school, New Age, but gets rejected. However, she doesn't give up. She has already written a few stories which she keeps in her drawer, stories nobody has even seen, but she will go ahead and follow her dream. So she starts writing for the high school newspaper, "The Nutmeg", signing her pieces with the mysterious name Pinky Weatherton. Her writings for the paper are sharp and pinpointing, which causes some waves in the school. Nobody knows who Pinky Weatherton is, and some people even assume that the mysterious writer is a guy. Then her dream comes true – she finally gets an invitation to join the New Age summer writing school, and she goes to New York to pursue her dream of becoming a writer.

One of her high school friends, George, encourages her more than anyone to follow a writing career. He says that she should write what she knows, write about people she knows, write about her life. So when she becomes a writer she will do just that – she will write her "Sex and the City" column, a column about her life and love experiences.

There are some differences between Carrie Bradshaw created by Candace Bushnell and Carrie Bradshaw created by the writers from "Sex and the City" the TV show. Carrie from "The Carrie Diaries" is still virgin in her high school senior year. Even though she dates Sebastian Kydd for months, she doesn't have sex with him, as she is reluctant to go so far in her relationship with him and start having sex, as opposed to her friends who have already done so. Although she is madly in love with Sebastian Kydd, she is not sure she should make such a commitment in her relationship with him. So when she goes to New York after graduating from high school, she is still virgin. In "Sex and the City" the show however, Carrie admits to Charlotte during season 3 that she had sex for the first time when she was in the 11th grade.

Another difference between Carrie Bradshaw from "The Carrie Diaries" and Carrie Bradshaw from "Sex and the City" the TV series is related to her family. In the book she lives with her father and the two sisters, and her mother is deceased. In the TV show, during season 4, she says that her father left her and her mother when she was 5 years old; also, no siblings are ever mentioned in the show.

Candace Bushnell herself was 19 years old when she first moved to New York to become a writer. So in a certain way, the story of Carrie Bradshaw is the story of her creator Candace Bushnell. While reading the book, I was wondering how much of Carrie's teen experiences were actually Candace Bushnell's own experiences. Was there such a kid, Sebastian Kydd, who was Candace Bushnell's boyfriend during high school years? Was there such a school paper, "The Nutmeg", where Candace Bushnell first started to write, before going to New York to become an acclaimed writer? Not impossible.

The end of the book is surprising. Carrie goes to New York to join the summer writing school, but she gets robbed the very first minute she sets foot in New York – someone steals her purse with all her money. She tries to contact George to ask for his help, but she can't reach him. Then she remembers that one of her friends from home, Donna LaDonna, gave her the number of her cousin from New York. So Carrie finds the phone number in the luggage, and calls this cousin of Donna's, who appears to be nobody else but Samantha Jones. I have to admit I just love the way the book ends. The two will become close friends, as expected, in the sequel book about the young Carrie Bradshaw, "Summer and the City".

"Summer and the City" by Candace Bushnell

By 2010 I had read all the six books published by Candace Bushnell up until that time – "Sex and the City", "Four Blondes", "Trading Up", "Lipstick Jungle", "One Fifth Avenue" and "The Carrie Diaries". I enjoyed all of them and they left me wanting for more. When I got to the last page of the last book, "The Carrie Diaries", I felt a sorrow for having read all of them and I wished there were more.

But what made me not be entirely sorrowful about it was the knowing that there *would* be more. When I found out about "The Carrie Diaries" sequel, "Summer and the City", I was excited at the prospect of reading yet another book by my favorite author Candace Bushnell, and I could hardly wait for it.

The book was released in April 2011, and I bought it on the very day when it first showed up in the bookstores. I enjoyed it so much!

Carrie Bradshaw is in New York now, attending writing classes and making her way to being a writer. New York City dazzles her with the beautiful parties, beautiful people, chic vintage stores and everything that is about the big city where the big success awaits her. Or maybe not? Turns out, becoming a writer is more difficult than she thought it would be. She has only 60 days of summer to make her dream come true, or she would have to face Brown College in fall. But she will not give up.

Meanwhile, her new life in New York City is so exciting, that she can't get enough of it. She met Samantha Jones, who helped her when she was robbed, and who promptly became her best friend (and her best teacher) in town. Guess what – Samantha Jones is engaged. Would you ever have thought of Samantha Jones being engaged to be married? Not in a million years! Yet she is. While reading the book, I was thinking – how come Samantha Jones is engaged??? This is SO NOT Samantha! Stay tuned.

Carrie gets lucky, as she finds her stolen purse. Turns out, the purse got dumped by the robbers, and a girl from New York found it along with Carrie's address book, so this girl calls Carrie to let her know about the purse. The two agree to meet in front of Saks; the purse finder says she can't be missed, as she has red hair. When I read "red hair", a flashbulb lightened in my head – Miranda, this must be her! So Carrie goes to Saks to meet the red-haired girl and get her purse back, but the young lady doesn't say her name. While reading this chapter, I was thinking, come on, wasn't this supposed to be Miranda? Some more suspense to the story… So I expected to find the red-haired girl in the next chapters, and there she was (when she and Carrie met again) – it really was Miranda, Carrie's second friend of the famous foursome.

By the end of the summer, Carrie is ready to do a reading event, when she would have a public listening to her newly written play for the first time. This is the chance she waited for, this is her opportunity to make it as a writer in New York. It depends on THIS if she is going to stay in New York and write, or go to Brown College.

So she reads her play in front of a number of people, but at the end it is not the way she expected it to be. Nobody seems impressed by her writing talents, so she decides to go back home, and then go to that dreaded college. But while on her way home, she gets a call inviting her to write a column in New York – her famous "Sex and the City" column in "New York

Star" newspaper, or "New York Observer" should we say? She made it, Carrie Bradshaw made it as a writer in New York!!!

When returning to New York to start her new life as a columnist, she meets Charlotte, who was reading "Brides" magazine (talking about Charlotte), and so the beloved foursome is complete – Carrie, Samantha, Miranda and Charlotte.

While reading the book, I enjoyed rediscovering some of the girls' stuff that we already knew from the previous "Sex and the City" books, TV shows and movies. Like Carrie's famous quote, "I can't help but wonder", a quote she used in her writing many times throughout the TV series and the two movies. Or Miranda snoring (remember Los Angeles in season 3 of the TV show, or Abu Dhabi in the second movie?). Or Samantha showing the finger at the beginning of "Summer and the City" the book, as well as in "Sex and the City" the second movie (the '80 memory flash). Also, Winnie Dieke, one of the characters from "Four Blondes", makes a cameo appearance in the book, as a journalist for "New York Post" who would cover Carrie's reading event. It is not the first time when Candace Bushnell's characters come back in the following books, this way making all her books related to one another as a whole epopee. And what about Samantha being engaged to be married? Forget about it, it will never happen!!! The engagement is broken and the wedding is called off, due to Samantha's faulty fallopian tubes. Of course she wouldn't get married, don't we know that about Samantha? So, no wonder her adversity for marriage and weddings throughout the whole "Sex and the City" story, after being rejected by her fiancé like this when she was in her twenties.

Of course, I noticed some differences between this new story about Carrie, and the other stories that we already knew –

"Sex and the City" the book from 1996, the TV series from 1998-2004, the two movies from 2008 and 2010. For instance, according to the second movie, Carrie meets her friends in New York in a different sequence (first Charlotte, then Miranda, then Samantha), as opposed to the other way around from "Summer and the City" the book, when she first meets Samantha, then Miranda, then Charlotte. Then Charlotte's story from "Sex and the City" the book published in 1996 is a bit different from "Summer and the City" written by Candace Bushnell and "Sex and the City" created by Michael Patrick King – there was Charlotte, the English journalist, as opposed to the totally American Charlotte. But who cares about little differences – read the book and enjoy it!

"Sleeping Arrangements" by Madeleine Wickham

"Sleeping Arrangements" is a funny book, featuring two families who don't know each over, but who get entangled together during a vacation in Spain, before an unexpected and unpredictable series of events develops.

The first family is Chloe, her long-time partner Philip Murray and their two teenage sons Sam and Nat. Chloe really needs a vacation, so she and Philip decide to accept their old friend Gerard's offer to spend a week in his luxurious villa in Spain. Besides, Philip has had some big troubles at work lately, so Chloe wants him to forget all about his work problems at least for a week and enjoy their upcoming vacation in Spain.

The second family is Hugh and Amanda Stratton, and their toddler daughters Beatrice and Octavia. Hugh has recently met his old friend, Gerard, and accepted his offer to spend a week in his luxurious villa from Spain. So the Stratton family head to the sunny peninsula for a nice vacation. They also bring along their daughters' nanny Jenna, who likes to make stupid jokes all the time, and laugh by herself at her own jokes.

When Chloe, Philip and their sons arrive at the destination, they are surprised to discover that the villa is already occupied by another family – the Strattons. Both families, who don't seem to have previously known one another, are consternated by this situation, and finally they realize that Gerard is their mutual friend and he must have double-booked the villa by mistake. So they come to the agreement to share the house for the week.

And so, an uneasy week of sharing and bumping into each other starts. But soon the reader discovers that the two families are not so strange to each over, like it seemed to be at the beginning of the story. When Hugh sees Chloe, he remembers an old flame which resurfaces again; and Chloe realizes she remembers Hugh all right, even though 15 years have elapsed since they last saw each over. The two of them end up to have a secret affair in the local hotel, and Hugh suddenly realizes he's not happy with his wife anymore, and that he actually wants Chloe back.

Then a casual remark made by some local kids force the two families to think deeper about their "casual" encounter at the Spanish villa, which is not so casual after all. If at the beginning of their vacation they think of one reason for all of them to be together in that villa, in the end they discover the real reason of their presence there is totally different, as someone has played a dirty and merciless game with them.

The "Shopaholic" Series by Sophie Kinsella

The "Shopaholic" series by British writer Sophie Kinsella (whose real name is Madeleine Wickham) is probably the most popular series of chick-lit books written since 2000. It's the story of the shopping addicted financial journalist Rebecca Bloomwood, a story which goes on throughout 6 novels of the series: "Confessions of a Shopaholic" (2000), "Shopaholic Takes Manhattan" (2001), "Shopaholic Ties the Knot" (2002), "Shopaholic and Sister" (2004), "Shopaholic and Baby" (2007) and "Mini Shopaholic" (2010).

The six "Shopaholic" novels focus on Becky's misadventures, as she has a pathologic shopping addiction and spends more money than she can actually afford. Throughout the novels, she gets in deep debts, but at the end of each book she manages to find a way to solve her financial issues. But did you think she gets any smarter? No, because in the next book her vicious spending starts all over again, bringing her into yet another financial disaster. And her problems are not only of financial nature. She is also a notorious liar, and because of that she gets into unbelievable troubles. The author really pushes her beyond any limits of common decency, making these books so hilarious and outrageously fun. Sometimes Becky is aggravating, but overall she is a nice girl.

The six "Shopaholic" books also focus on the development of Becky's relationship with Luke Brandon: she falls in love with him, then they start dating, get married, have a baby.

A movie loosely based on "Shopaholic" series by Sophie Kinsella was released in February 2009, starring Isla Fisher as Rebecca Bloomwood. The film, titled "Confessions of a Shopaholic", was a relatively big success.

ACKNOWLEGEMENTS

Thank you,

To Irina Apostu, author of "Touristic Vancouver", who supported and helped me along the process – your input, suggestions and patience were invaluable.

To my beloved family and friends who believed in me and encouraged me to write – this book wouldn't have been possible without you.

To all my readers who have been by my side since the first day I started to write – I couldn't have been a writer if it weren't for you.

www.ingramcontent.com/pod-product-compliance
Lightning Source LLC
Chambersburg PA
CBHW030846180526
45163CB00004B/1469

*9 7 8 1 4 9 2 3 1 6 3 4 3 *